FURNISHING A
COUNTRY COTTAGE

FURNISHING A COUNTRY COTTAGE

JOHN WOODFORDE

Introduction by
Audrey Powell

**DAVID & CHARLES
NEWTON ABBOT**

ISBN 0 7153 5748 4

COPYRIGHT NOTICE

© JOHN WOODFORDE 1972

All rights reserved. No part of this publication may be reproduced, stored in a retrieval system, or transmitted, in any form or by any means, electronic, mechanical, photocopying, recording or otherwise, without the prior permission of David & Charles (Publishers) Limited

Set in eleven on thirteen point Baskerville
and printed in Great Britain
by W J Holman Limited Dawlish
for David & Charles (Publishers) Limited
South Devon House Newton Abbot Devon

Contents

chapter		page
	List of Illustrations	7
	Introduction by Audrey Powell	9
1	Empty rooms	15
2	Intrusions	21
3	Floors and staircases	26
4	Walls, grates and shelves	31
5	The kitchen	42
6	Bedrooms	53
7	The sitting room	61
8	The dining room	71
9	The bathroom	79
10	The spare room	87
11	The study	92
12	Buying furniture	96

13	The garden	107
14	The coming of cottage furniture	112
15	Furnishing to let	124
	Acknowledgements	129
	Index	131

List of Illustrations

PLATES

Regency cottage and its white interior	33
Timbered cottages *(courtesy of King and Chasemore, estate agents, Horsham, Sussex)*	34
Uniform carpet and curtain treatment	34
Sitting room with bookshelves	51
Dining room	52
Fireplaces *(photograph of hob grate by courtesy of Dr Johnson's House Trust)*	85
Bedroom and bathroom	86
Interior of an unimproved cottage *(courtesy of Popperfoto Library)*	103
Kitchens *(photograph of old kitchen by courtesy of Popperfoto Library)*	104

DRAWINGS AND ENGRAVINGS

Cottage curtains of the 1830s †	36
Round table, from *Plain Man's Guide to Second-Hand Furniture*, Frank Davis *(courtesy of Michael Joseph)*	39
Bureau bookcase *	39
Victorian grate, from Coalbrookdale catalogue, 1875 *(courtesy of County Life Books)*	40
Stone-flagged kitchen	44
Windsor chairs for a kitchen *	47
Cottage furniture of the 1830s †	49
Chest of drawers †	57
Box toilet glasses *	58
Tables for a sitting room *	66
Colour Wheel, from *Making the Most of Colour in the Home*, W. Alan Taylor *(courtesy of Arco Publications)*	67
American cottage sofas ¶	68
Table for a dining room *	72
Chairs for a dining room *	74

Modern Windsor and wing chair, from *English Furniture* by Barbara Jones *(courtesy of The Architectural Press)*	75
Washstands *	88
Reading chair ¶	94
Box divan in octagonal room ¶	95
Italian-style cottage †	113
Multi-purpose table †	114
American cottage furniture for bedrooms ¶	116
Sofa-bed †	118
Straw firescreen †	119
New England cottage ¶	121

Engravings marked † are from J. C. Loudon's *Encyclopaedia of Cottage, Farm and Villa Architecture*, 1833

Drawings marked * are by Roy Spencer from John Woodforde's *The Observer's Book of Furniture (courtesy of Frederick Warne)*

Engravings marked ¶ are from A. J. Downing's *Architecture of Country Houses*, 1850

The drawing on page 44 and the end pieces to certain chapters are by Rex Whistler, from *A Thatched Roof* by Beverley Nichols *(courtesy of Jonathan Cape)*

Introduction

The calendar over my desk shows a cottage with its long, low, rough white walls snuggling into a Norfolk reed thatch as thick as a new broom.

Studying the photograph a thought struck me—which a quick check confirmed—that all the other eleven cottages in the calendar were also photographed from the outside. Lifting the phone I rang a firm which produces that sort of calendar. Did they ever use cottage photographs taken indoors? I asked. They seemed surprised: 'Oh no, always outsides'. Why? 'Because they are usually a lot more attractive than the interiors', came the reply.

Obviously John Woodforde is not alone in believing there is need for guidance on cottage furnishing.

I am reminded of 'the judge's cottage', the outside of which looked so uninteresting in the illustration on the agent's particulars that it was days before I arranged to see it. Yet inside it proved to be the most comfortably and tastefully furnished cottage I have been in. Nothing was new, or of great value, but the carpets on the crooked staircases blended so well with the curtains. The walls of bookshelves merged with the beams; the deep armchairs

Introduction

looked as though they were part of the great inglenook; the quaint bedrooms were arranged to make the most of the slanting floors and blackened posts.

I would have bought it, lock, stock and water-barrel. But it was already under offer.

Years later it turned up on the market again. What a disappointment. Now there was a jazzy modern unit in the big kitchen, and in every room were different colours, floor coverings, types of furniture. The mellowness and tranquillity had gone with the previous owner, and so had the property's appeal. You felt that owner had loved it, and this one had just lived in it.

A cottage is such a personal thing. Leslie Dunkling, author of *English House Names*, notes that local authority tenants seldom name their houses, nor are names given to flats. But nearly all cottages are named.

Along with winning the pools and living on a desert island, owning a cottage must be the English town dweller's most cherished dream. His summer version has bees humming round hollyhocks and delphiniums in the garden, the scent of stocks and pinks drifting in through the open lattice. The winter edition has the roof crisply capped with snow, woodsmoke curling from the chimney, and a warm fireglow showing through the curtained windows. But ask him to describe the inside and he is at a loss.

Perhaps subconsciously he skates over niggling memories of childhood stays in cottages—the fourposter bed, with wooden rings that rattled as the curtains were pulled, making animal-head shadows on the walls in the candlelight. But it is convenient to forget the coldness of that bedroom in winter, the sticky, oily-smelling linoleum—and all that paraphernalia of cans of hot water in the morning.

Cottages themselves come in all shapes and sizes, ages and conditions. John Woodforde describes over fifty types

Introduction

in an earlier book, *The Truth about Cottages*, illustrated in detail by Bertha Stamp.

Certainly one would want to furnish a jettied Tudor antiquity lurching over some Suffolk village street differently from the way one would want to breathe character into the rooms of a rugged granite box, built for durability rather than beauty, on a Cornish moor.

You would think in different terms again, looking for the right things for a stylish little Cotswold stone home. The trim Georgian town cottage with its sash windows and well-proportioned rooms would absorb a type of furniture which would look entirely out of place in some converted fisherman's home in the West Country. Here you could expect painters' canvasses and all-purpose divans to be the main equipment.

In these days when everyone, from duke to hippie, may at times choose to be a cottage dweller, the range of interior treatment you come upon is endless.

There are plastic flowers and flickering television sets which seem to be the only furnishing you see in some rooms as you walk down a village street. But for these families a cottage is just a roof. They would move to a neo-Georgian tomorrow if they could.

The true cottage addict will try to make the inside as interesting as he can—in his own fashion. I know one who covered the living room walls with paper-backed hessian used for packaging—and he could have done much worse. Another painted all the downstairs walls bright red—and with the plentiful dark oak beams it did not look too bad.

Another turned a windowless room, of the kind you sometimes get when two buildings are made into one, into a bedroom—contrary to regulations, of course. Walls, floor and ceiling were painted black. He (an architect, by the way) added two Spanish-style beds, like upturned

11

Introduction

tables, painted white, and white Japanese lanterns. As the finishing touch, a trumpet—for what reason I never knew—was hung from the ceiling.

You don't come upon such originality often—which is probably a good thing. But, if the owner has money to spare, you may get glossy wood-block flooring, modern wrought-iron panels down the staircase, a priest's hole turned into a mirrored cocktail bar, and a picture-window at the back looking out on the swimming pool. Which is all a little sad because the owner's real habitat is obviously a 1970s ranch-house.

Cottages do seem to bring out the ingeniousness in people, perhaps of necessity, or possibly because it is ingenious people who buy them. Owners are marvellous at 'inventing' space for the innumerable paids of garden boots the family possesses; for large baskets for large dogs; for racks for the wine they make as a hobby... And they take pride in things found on the premises—the grinding stone dug up by the builders, a carving found in a wall, or some bit of statuary salvaged from the well.

Sometimes you long to alter something that jars in an otherwise thoughtful modernisation—glass handles or flush doors, where a simple latch door was called for. Some off-the-peg wardrobe units seem too slick in a bedroom where the floors creak and the window dips. A costly fireplace bears no relationship to the age of the building, while an original one is boarded up in another room to make a china cupboard. Windows get mixed as replacements are made over the years, cheap fletton bricks 'won't show' at the back—but they do. Simulated-wood kitchen units have the falseness of the material emphasised when set against the oak or pine furniture John Woodforde so rightly recommends.

Before I stop being bitchy I must not forget the sort of cottages (and I have an actress's in mind), where they are

Introduction

determined to do the 'real thing', until the place drips with olde worldiness. Doors are all china fingerplates, and the bedrooms so smothered in sprigged paper on walls and ceilings, with matching curtains, blinds and bed covers, that you can scarcely find your way out.

John Woodforde makes no outlandish furnishing suggestions—all are within the range and pocket of the average owner. He just throws out ideas as he leads you on a leisurely conducted cottage tour. They should set the uncertain owner on the right path leaving him free to express his own personality with his final choice. Obviously you won't agree with the author in everything, but if you are interested enough to read this sort of book you will probably go along with him much of the way.

Once you have got cottages in your blood and managed to get one of your own, furnishing it should be an agreeable chore. It is less harrowing than watching builders pull the place to pieces, less exhausting than doing this yourself. It is something to look forward to, after that stage is over, and prevents an anti-climax.

The attractions of cottage-furnishing are that it need not be an expensive hobby, you can pick up bits in your own good time and at whatever price you can afford. And it is a hobby you can indulge in anywhere. You can take home a piece of glass from an Edinburgh shop as a souvenir of your Scottish holiday; or acquire a set of old fire-irons or a lace-maker's chair and bring them back in the car from a tour of France or Spain. And when you are tired of a piece, you may be able to sell it and improve on it. Anyway, it gives you an excuse to potter round antique shops and junk stores, and attend sales.

There are books in plenty about cottages, but never too many. We who subscribe to the cult read them all gladly, always hoping for new ideas to try, just as we never cease

Introduction

to enjoy going over other cottages to see how this owner turned his hall into a dining area, or by what means—whether with ribbons, or dolls, miniatures or little velvet cushions—he gives visitors warning of the low beams and doorways on which he has so often banged his own head in the past.

A.P.
July 1972

CHAPTER 1

Empty rooms

Having done up your country cottage, wait a little before you enter the final stage of making it habitable. The rooms may be intact now, swept out and smilingly empty, but are you sure damp patches are not reasserting themselves? Is there perhaps a faggot oven or another inglenook you would like to unblock? Have you really got enough power points? Equally important, do you now notice that a mantleshelf or a door frame has been set on a slant where it should be level, or officially level where a slight slope or bend would fit in with the rest of the features?

Opportunities for adjusting such things are only obvious sometimes when all is filled and painted, a point it might be tactful to make to your builder (in roughly those words) when asking him to do part of his work all over again.

The sort of cottage I have in mind, I should say, has no more than three small bedrooms and a date between 1700 and 1900. Few labourers' cottages have survived over two hundred years; so if yours is very old it is probably an ex-farmhouse—or a part of a farmhouse. Whether you already possess some furniture or must start buying from scratch,

15

Empty rooms

there will be numerous questions to ask yourself. It can be an enjoyable preliminary to wander alone about the cottage, feeling the rooms, taking in their shapes, measuring places where certain items might go and noting access up the stairs.

Now is the time to put some curtains in the windows. They needn't be your final choice of curtain. The point is that even old sheets held by tacks suggest occupation and deter young stone-throwers: once I was sitting on the floor of an empty cottage miles from a village when a flint tinkled through a window pane and landed at my feet. I got outside in time to see two boys disappearing fast on bicycles.

It may occur to you, especially if you are studying your cottage at night with the aid of a candle, that the bare rooms look so graceful and inviting that it's a pity they have to be furnished at all. Barristers and BBC announcers of the 1930s, responding to this thought, tended to furnish their weekend cottages with too little too carefully arranged. Osbert Lancaster invented the label 'cultured cottage'. In *Homes Sweet Homes*, 1939, he drew and described its typically prim interior decked out with specimens of peasant handicraft, hand-painted rhyme sheets and a rag paper edition of *A Shropshire Lad* accidentally conspicuous on a small artist-designed table of Elizabethan oak.

But few furnishers today need to be warned about sparsity or about that other extreme, stifling clutter. The coming of the cultured cottage in its various forms has helped to bring back a sensible pre-Victorian simplicity to the insides of restored cottages. It is a simplicity radically different from the old. Where the cottager of 150 years ago spaced out his furniture because of poverty, his modern successor spaces out for a comfortable effect; he is prepared to prune well-liked possessions to avoid spoiling a room whose arrangement of doors and stairs shows that it was never intended to hold much furniture.

The choice of pieces for an old cottage should perhaps be a compromise, a mixture of old and new, of antiques and of stripped or painted junk, and all hard-wearing and practical. The notion of bringing back a genuine cottage interior of two centuries ago, based on the cottage necessities listed in old inventories, is recognised now as no more than a talking-point; though certainly a Victorian cottage barely 100 years old might take well to a preponderance of mid-Victorian mahogany: smaller balloon-back chairs, solid oval tables with rounded edges, a secretaire bookcase. In *any* cottage it might be affected to introduce high-back settles and box beds—both designed to mitigate extreme draughts—and such museum objects as skillets, carriage lamps, horse brasses and spinning wheels.

To bring in only things which are useful seems to be an adequate rule of thumb. If you want some antique country-made articles, select ones you can use; plenty of them remain as serviceable as when the craftsman gave them his final pat of the hand and if they aren't they can be mended. Ornaments and pictures qualify, of course, where they usefully and pleasingly decorate the space between, say, the fireplace and the ceiling.

A carriage lamp may well in itself be decorative, having its parts ornamentally fashioned, but it was no more made for lighting a porch than horse brasses for drawing attention to the beam above an inglenook. Spinning wheels may be beautifully formed, but they were not meant to stand functionless in a cottage room. It's a matter of judgement. Obviously a pair of antique brass candlesticks would usefully provide light, and a jug of beaten copper could have some point if used to hold flowers, or adapted, with the least mutilation, to act as a table lamp.

It is different if you collect and study carriage lamps, horse brasses and spinning wheels. The advantage, though, of collecting things never meant to have more than visual appeal—things like busts, china figures, paintings and prints—is that there is not much difficulty about displaying them. Be careful, of course, about displaying them at all in a cottage occupied only at weekends. Do it where you normally live and wait until the cottage becomes your home. Taking an antiquarian's interest in minor works of art (who made them, when, where and why?) often becomes an absorbing occupation to people who settle down in a country cottage. A visit to a public library will show that there is no shortage of books for specialist collectors.

I am assuming that you have running water and electricity (a village cottage may have gas) and thus the wherewithal, at the touch of a switch, to produce warmth in your rooms and immersion-heated water from your taps. The upper section of a bedroom cupboard, containing a heated water tank, is ideal for airing linen and clothes. A central heating system is, I suggest, a needlessly elaborate amenity for a small cottage. The advantage of instant heating with separate appliances is that you use only the heat you want at a particular time; maintaining a nice warm cottage when there is no one there to enjoy it merely wastes power and over-dries the furniture.

Convected heat can be supplied by slim, oil-filled radiators plugged into normal 13-amp power points. They resemble the hot-water radiators that go with central heating and can be thermostatically controlled from room to room. For radiant heat, the sort which travels in a straight line and warms whatever it strikes, there is a range of electric fires whose red hot coil can be looked at with pleasure on a cold day. Then, of course, there are the mysteries of off-peak storage heating which you may like to look into. But I hope

Empty rooms

that, despite all these electrical amenities, you will put some reliance on open fireplaces and take advantage of living outside the smokeless zones.

But something should be said of country cottages without running water and electricity, of cottages where it would be uneconomic to lay them on. The British Isles still contain thousands, some of them down farm tracks within a few miles of London; and if your cottage is one of them, or if you are thinking of buying one, don't imagine that life will be impossible without the installation of a powered pump or the plant for generating electricity.

Oil lamps and paraffin heaters are very efficient and candles are the cheapest of today's luxury goods. Paraffin heaters which are actually attractive may be hard to find, but oil lamps and their shades can be as handsome as any electric table lamp; and they have the merit that every part, including the bulbous base, serves a purpose. There is the temptation, indeed, for the cottager with electricity thrust upon him to fit up his oil lamps with flex and bulb: such lamps are certainly likely to please him for a longer period than open grates supplied with fake fuel and electrically simulated flames.

One of my favourite cottages is a former Hertfordshire gamekeeper's (c 1800) set by itself in a valley beside a small river and approached only by an estate track which winds and undulates through woodland. It has three bedrooms and has been charmingly furnished by the man who now lives there, a collector of old glass and microscopes. By any official rating, it is sub-standard.

There is neither electricity nor running water—not even a tap. Yet the kitchen has a modern cooker and a refrigerator, both worked by bottled gas (the gas could provide lighting, too, but this cottage has oil lamps). Water comes from a spout over the sink in response to pressure of hand

19

Empty rooms

or elbow on the pump handle. The bath is portable, of course, but there is a water closet containing a well-seated long hopper flushed by means of a pail of water standing by.

It is true that the cottage strikes cold on returning to it in winter, but a great contrast is produced in a few minutes when wood and coal fires are alight in two communicating rooms. An advantage of a fire in each room is that the draughts inevitably drawn are warm draughts.

A centuries-old complaint about open fires is that they roast you on one side and leave you shivering on the other—a criticism which has more to do with spacious houses than cottages. In the cottage I refer to, the wall opposite the sitting-room fire is near enough to absorb and throw back the warmth. A thermometer hangs on this wall. One bitter winter's night I noticed, while listening to the proprietor playing a waltz on his harmonium, that the temperature was 88°F.

Whatever the shape of a country cottage—vernacular and low-ceilinged, classically symmetrical or carefully old English—the kind of retreat I have in mind holds out a promise of peace, seclusion, intimacy and happy days of pottering about. There is magic still, perhaps more now than ever, in the phrase 'cottage in the country'.

CHAPTER 2
Intrusions

In these pages I am imagining that your cottage is rather more than a weekend retreat, and that when you have to be away someone will keep an eye on the place. No building having windows and doors is secure against a determined intruder; and an unoccupied cottage may fall easy prey, especially when out of sight from other buildings.

Vandals might inflict damage or perhaps only make a mess, but a professional thief, knowing which things are worth taking, would load up his van accordingly. You will doubtless have insurance cover for theft as well as fire, but valuable antiques, collector's items, silver, porcelain, old masters or jewellery should not be left in an unoccupied cottage. Ask the milkman not to put milk on the doorstep when he knows you are away. A letterbox of adequate size will discourage the postman and newsagent from leaving letters and papers sticking out until your return.

People breaking in are not the only hazard. Mice are particularly unwelcome. All holes that could possibly admit them should be blocked up (though not with newspaper), and ground-level ventilation points checked to ensure they

Intrusions

have not become damaged by rust. Mice already inhabiting the cottage can be effectively dealt with by cheese-baited traps; proprietary poisons unfortunately leave corpses in unreachable places to signal their existence for weeks.

Nature presses in upon a country cottage. All kinds of animals have their habitats just outside; and so do birds, which are liable to claw and peck at thatch and block gutter pipes with nesting materials. A bird slipping down the chimney may cause major damage, perhaps sweeping ornaments off shelves; to prevent this, fit a piece of thick wire mesh, heavily galvanised against corrosion, over the chimney pots. Furniture beetles, which cause the well-known worm holes, breed among the dead branches of coppices and can hardly be prevented from flying in at cottage windows, along with hornets, horseflies and pond-bred mosquitoes. Wasps and bees may select your roof space or a cavity behind the wall tiles as a site for a potentially irruptive nest.

An aerosol insecticide, sparingly used, is invaluable for killing flies, while a jar half full of watery jam placed on an outside sill will divert wasps from coming indoors and trap them. Intruding ants can be exasperating. You can kill them off by the hundred and yet, when you enter the kitchen next morning, there they are again, blackly swarming on a draining board or shelf. Ants like to breed in the mortar of old buildings, and get inside through minute crevices: an opening only one-sixteenth of an inch allows free movement to most insect pests. Watch the ants to see from which direction they come. It may be necessary to pull out a firmly fixed piece of kitchen equipment to find the crack in the wall or floor which they are using; but once you have plugged it with cement you will have no more trouble. In the meantime ants can be prevented from reaching uncovered food by standing its container in a bowl of water. Putting down the sort of poison bait which is supposed to wipe out the whole colony through the ants carrying the stuff back to the nest is, in my experience, a waste of time.

Keeping out things that are not wanted is a constant concern in any country cottage. Moisture rising up from the ground is one of the more unpleasant invaders, not only because of the centipedes and silver fish it is inclined to attract. Make sure that there are no mounds of earth up against the walls, the result of a tendency for flower beds to rise: it could be that reducing the level of the ground to below that of the floor inside is all that need be done to eliminate dampness.

The old way of dealing with rising damp was wall-boarding (discussed as a decorative feature in chapter 4), but today there are several waterproof compositions and sheetings which may be close-fitted as a treatment for areas of persistent dampness. Properly applied, they prevent water from reaching the surface. However, if a wall is treated on both sides, this may have unfortunate results, because then the water cannot evaporate and is forced to climb ever higher.

A treatment suitable in particular cases (it fortifies the function of guttering) is a trench dug round the cottage, lined with concrete which slopes outwards, and with holes in a brief retaining wall through which the water drains away. Digging in a damp course all round the building is an extremely expensive remedy and, with thick walls, almost impossible to carry out effectively.

But sometimes damp patches in non-cavity walls are due to a porous brick, for it is not uncommon for a brick or two in a thousand to have lost—or never to have had—adequate water-resisting qualities. If the face of any outside brick has flaked off, and there is an ugly stain within

Intrusions

the building, it may seem that the brick ought to be replaced.

Compared with rising damp, the entry of rain water should be easily prevented—by repairing the roof. Give special care to its joints with the chimney stack and deal with such insidious water traps as those produced by leaky down-pipes from gutters.

Major damage to your furniture and carpets would be caused by a burst pipe left to flow unchecked. Make a habit of turning off the main stopcock when you go away. It may be advisable—and some insurance companies demand it—to turn off mains power as well.

The penetration of glare and excessive heat into your cottage during warm weather may be the consequence of a window having been 'opened up', making it too large for a particular room: in strong sunlight a picture window facing south can easily send the temperature into the 90s. One remedy, other than rebuilding the window, is to install louvered shutters or slatted blinds which pleasantly filter the light and inhibit the cucumber-frame action of plate glass. Shutters also help to keep out the cold.

Draughts are a most annoying intrusion, adding greatly to the heat loss of a room, since warmed air is pushed out elsewhere; draughts hurry in beneath and round doors, through the crevices at window joints and the cracks between floorboards. These vulnerable points should be plugged or fitted with draught excluders of a suitable kind. There is no need to worry about lack of ventilation: you are unlikely to block every draught so perfectly that a supply of air is entirely excluded. This point can be proved if a solid fuel fire will burn without sending smoke into the room.

Draughts can also be eliminated by the installation of double-glazing, which at the same time reduces noise. The intrusion of noise may not at first be associated with life in the country, but unfortunately thousands of cottages stand beside busy roads and in village streets carrying heavy traffic. Back windows as well as those at the front should be double-glazed for protection.

Some old cottages, however, have thick, solid walls, providing a sound barrier which is missing in modern buildings. The heavier a construction in relation to its thickness, the less sound penetrates; so a 9in wall of solid bricks or stones is a much better defence than a wall of lightweight blocks or of studwork covered with laths and plaster.

The sound of near neighbours' transistor radios, television sets and record-players can be a problem, which is not to be solved by covering your walls with a sound-absorbing material like glass fibre quilt; the function of this is not to stop noise coming in but to reduce it by absorption in the room where it originates. (If you are yourself a hi-fi addict, the point is worth considering, before your neighbours in turn complain). Where a party wall in a terrace or semi-detached cottage proves an inadequate barrier, the only satisfactory form of soundproofing is to give it an extra skin—with no chinks in it—of a solid material like brick or concrete. But one good thing about noise from next door, which cannot be said of the other intruders I have mentioned, is that in response to a polite request it will sometimes go away.

CHAPTER 3

Floors and staircases

Although work may already have been carried out on the floors, look at them carefully before the final stages are reached for there may still be adjustments to make. Have you overlooked, for instance, having a shallow well for the door mat to stop it slipping and fraying?

As you go over the cottage now, especially if it is seventeenth century and timber-framed, it may be even more noticeable than before how much the bedroom floors slope. You could, of course, ask the builder to lay false floors which are level, but I suggest you leave sloping floors as they are—there is no danger where the main structure is sound—and just arrange that the furniture stands level. Sloping tables are hard to get used to and sloping beds impossible.

A usual procedure is to rest the legs of the furniture on squares of wood, suitably graded, though this leaves the articles free to slip with a bump if slightly moved. It is better, when the position of the furniture has been decided on, to attach small blocks of wood to the base of each item, so allowing them to move together. Fixed with bone glue (which is melted by water), or with a screw, they can be readily removed if necessary. Needless to say, a little time-consuming work is needed to adjust the levelling blocks to the right thickness.

One of the things to look out for is loose floor boards; this entails treading on each board separately. It's well worth driving in extra nails, since squeaks and thumps do not disappear with time; indeed they tend to grow louder, and are particularly irritating when sealed away under a layer of close-fitting carpet.

If several boards sag under your weight, a wall plate or the end of a joist may have become rotten and will have to be repaired. This trouble is common in the downstairs rooms of old cottages whose floor boards were put in on top of an earth floor and allowed no proper ventilation. Often such boards are not worth keeping and the builder may already have replaced them with 6in of concrete.

To renovate brick or flagstone floors, it may be necessary, for the sake of dryness, to re-lay on concrete, or to renew cement joins. Brick tends to look dusty, however well washed, so it is best to glaze or wax polish it.

Before covering floor boards upstairs, you might consider cleaning them and leaving them on view. After abrasion with a sanding machine, the most sordid boards can become an attractive asset, especially those cut from oak or one of the fruit woods; if they are then coated with a sealing fluid, little polishing of the surface will be necessary.

There is also a lot to be said for painting boards in gloss black; even the dullest-looking are transformed instantly at a cost of a few pence. Be sure to sweep away all surface dust and grit before you start painting; dirt in the cracks can be an advantage, however, because paint applied liberally will bind it into a solid filling and stifle any penetrating draughts.

Floors and staircases

An important decision to make is whether to have the floors covered by carpets or rush matting, or left polished and strewn with rugs. In some cottages an effective result can be achieved by treating the various divisions, including the hall and stairs, as a continuous area with a single colour running right through. Where there are small rooms leading out of one another, the trick is to avoid too much variety; repeated changes in colour, pattern and texture can be an irritation to the eye. You might consider having a centre carpet in each room of an identical colour, with the floor surrounds in a single colour as well. Carpets within a surround do tend, however, to reduce the apparent size of a room, the line of vision being interrupted in three places: where the carpet meets the surround, where the surround meets the bottom of the skirting board and where the top of the skirting board meets the wall.

Although wall-to-wall carpeting may cost considerably more than an individual carpet and will not last so well as it cannot be turned to distribute wear, nevertheless it gives more comfort and warmth as well as greater convenience when cleaning. Depending on a wise choice of colour and pattern, fitted Wilton or Axminster carpet will not look out of place in an old cottage and may add considerably to its well-being. Some of the modern designs and carpets of synthetic fibre are obviously better suited to a modern flat.

In rooms with fitted carpets, it is usually necessary to saw a strip off the bottom of doors to give clearance for the carpet and its felt underlay, but as cottage floors are often uneven or slope, it may be necessary to saw in an uneven line to get a door to open fully without scraping the pile, thereby spoiling its appearance. The answer to this is an ingenious device known as the rising butt hinge, whose spiral form causes a door to rise as it opens, thus clearing the carpet however closely it fits when shut. Rising butts have additional advantages: the spirals gently impel an open door to swing shut; and, since the two parts of the hinge slot together, a door can be lifted from its frame without the aid of a screwdriver.

Rush matting looks well on some cottage floors, especially where white wall plaster is mixed with structural timbers of natural oak; it is also ideal for covering stone passages, tiled or brick floors and bare boards. It comes in a variety of patterns and can be bought in different sizes with additional 1ft squares which, when joined, will fit into awkward corners. Rush and straw matting is relatively inexpensive, and easily taken up so that floors can be swept.

Rugs on polished floors add greatly to the decorative appearance of a room. Apart from traditionally-designed or plain thickly-piled rugs of English manufacture, there are many attractive and unusual ones imported from India, Spain and the Scandinavian countries, which would add colour and originality to the right setting. The shape of a rug, too, plays an effective part in the arrangement of a room; for instance, placed under a round table, a square rug may look better than a rectangular one.

The choice of hard finishes for floors is wide. There are quarry tiles, ceramic tiles, lino and plastic tiles, tinted concrete squares sealed with polyurethane and cork squares sealed with polyvinyl; there are also wooden parquet shapes of various thicknesses, some of them being very thin and mounted on small sheets of plywood. But I am not anxious to recommend such materials except in the kitchen and bathroom, for they tend to suggest the feel of a modern house or bungalow. Beware of simulated natural materials; in the confines of an old cottage, they are quickly seen to be bogus especially when placed alongside the genuine article.

Where a kitchen is to have a floor covering of vinyl, lino

Floors and staircases

or plastic tiles, these should ideally be laid beforehand so that heavy equipment can be set on top of them—a more efficient procedure than having to fit the material round the equipment. If lino, whether in tile or sheet form, is to cover a boarded floor, an underlay of hardboard will prevent the ridges of the boards from showing through.

The staircase is something you are bound to have to think about. In some cottages, it may be a space-saving spiral of stone or cast iron; should you have this sort, you will no doubt value it for its antiquity and workmanship and make light of having to remove an upper window to bring in the bedroom furniture. Carpeting is hardly suitable on stone or metal treads; but there should be a particularly firm hand rail all the way up. In practice, spiral staircases are no more dangerous than a flight with just a few winders: all the treads are the same shape and you quickly become accustomed to the rhythm of turning.

Spiral and semi-spiral staircases are normally enclosed by a door and situated in a kitchen or living room between the chimney stack and an outside wall. When made of wood—perhaps elm—they are sometimes moved to a place considered more convenient. You may prefer to leave them where they are. Unless the wooden treads are of interesting quality—polished oak, for example—they are best covered in pile carpet. Haircord, in a range of colours, wears well on a staircase, but tends to be more slippery. Unless the stairs are to be close-fitted, the ends of the treads should first be painted—white gloss brightens poorly-lit corners.

In laying staircarpet, remember that it mostly comes in widths of 27in and 36in, and the treads of a straight flight are unlikely to be narrower than 30in or wider than 33in. Lay the carpet up the middle of the stairs on pieces of underfelt, fixing it with tacks at the back of each tread and also, though more sparingly, beneath the lips of the treads.

CHAPTER 4

Walls, grates and shelves

If you have yet to decorate your walls, or are now uncertain about the colours, why not whitewash everything—and take in all but the very low overhead beams? This is what many cottagers have always done; only there are now tins of smooth emulsion paint instead of whitewash. But don't overdo it. During a craze for white in the early 1930s, even good chairs and tables were painted white; they still turn up in auction salerooms with antique walnut or mahogany showing through the paint.

Obviously white is not the only basic colour, but you would find it does not clash with anything, makes the easiest of backgrounds to live with and is friendly to come home to. There are many subtle variations of pure white —tints of magnolia, primrose, aquamarine, for instance— which may look equally attractive with other furnishings you have in mind.

If you want the plastered part of the walls grey or a soft orange or blue, you will need large areas of white paint, and certainly white skirting boards, to act as a foil. You could, of course, whiten only the plaster and have the

Walls, grates and shelves

woodwork brown. But remember that in deciding to have brown skirting, which would wear a little better than white, you at once limit your choice of carpet.

Cream-coloured paint and distemper have been much used for being less dazzling and somehow more refined than white; but cream without the contrast of white alongside has a half-hearted, dingy look and can even make a room appear shapeless.

Don't worry about the dazzle of white surfaces. There won't be any to speak of by the time your rooms have furniture and fittings for the eye to rest on. Pictures and lamp brackets break up wall surfaces, as do pieces of furniture standing against them, and shelves of books and ornaments. The shiny whiteness of panelled doors can be agreeably relieved by suitable door furniture: knobs, keyhole covers, even finger plates, of brass or porcelain. The older ledged and braced doors are better fitted with simple iron latches, painted black or dark grey, or the wooden kind operated on one side with a bootlace or cord. Curtains, drawn or undrawn, have a softening effect, especially where they can successfully be allowed to hang from near the ceiling right down to the floor.

Let me say a word or two about the hanging of curtains. There are several ingenious curtain rails on the market and rufflette tape has long been a blessing to all; but there is now a fashion (which I like) for disposing of pelmets and hanging the curtains from large rings on a thick curtain rod. This is not a new idea; it is an early nineteenth-century revival—see the illustration of 1830 curtains on p 36 and compare with those shown on p 34. Today, though, the rod is set higher to ensure light exclusion and the tops of curtains are reinforced by a three-inch band of canvas. Incidentally, rings run better if the rod is smoothed with a silicone polish.

Page 33
Regency cottage:
(above) a familiar simple type;
(below) the white walls and doors of its interior

Page 34 Timbered cottages: *(above)* Seventeenth-century farmhouse divided long ago into three cottages; note off-centre chimney stack; *(below)* uniform carpet and curtain treatment draws two small rooms into one. In foreground, ladder-back rocker

Many cottage-owners like to have flowered wallpaper, particularly in the bedrooms. Some papers, ready glazed and therefore impervious to water vapour, add colour and warmth to a bathroom. It is certainly a traditional material, anything up to ten layers having been found on old cottage walls. Until the latter part of the nineteenth century, however, it was less used in downstairs rooms than whitewash because it wouldn't hold properly on damp patches and showed mould marks.

There are plenty of other interesting wall coverings on the market; but most of them would look more at home in a new bungalow than an old cottage. I would hesitate to recommend painted fabrics, ribbed acoustic tiles, paper-backed cork squares, panels of mosaic tiling, flock papers with a velvet finish, quilted or satin papers, pegboard, sections of imitation stone, Japanese grasscloth, leatherette, a sheeting called lincrustin which resembles wood or masonry, or a sheeting called wickertrim which looks like wickerwork. To form an idea of the incongruity of certain up-to-date wall finishes, it is only necessary to glance at the decor of a village pub on which the brewers have lavished the full modernising treatment.

If your cottage was once a small farmhouse or manor, it is possible that the walls of at least one downstairs room are covered with framed panels; originally pale green, blue or putty colour, they may have been painted a dark chocolate in Victorian times. By all means keep them, so long as probing has revealed nothing serious in the way of wet rot: the smallest infestation of *dry* rot, which crazes wood, smells foul and spreads alarmingly, would mean removing floors and joists, let alone the panelling itself. Treat good panels with respect; they are rare in a cottage. If you find that the wood is oak or one of the hardwoods, try to bring out the natural colour to the best advantage. One treatment would

Walls, grates and shelves

Curtains recommended for cottages in the 1830s. The heavy pole and rings returned to favour in the 1970s. Compare p 34

be to clean down, rub with linseed oil, wait until dry, then polish over with wax.

The panelling, or wainscoting, had a purpose beyond that of good appearance and heat retention. It dealt most effectively with one of the chief evils that beset small domestic buildings, the dark mouldy patches caused by rising damp; cavity walls and damp courses were almost unknown until the nineteenth century. Panelling provided both the insulation of a cavity wall and the disappearance from sight and feel of moist areas. The drawback was that after a period of years the hardwood battens tended to rot. Where these remain in good order, it may be found that the main source of rising damp in the walls has been reduced by the addition at some time of guttering—this can take away much of the rainwater which otherwise soaks in beside the footings of a building.

An attractive form of wainscoting sometimes seen in old cottages is the sort which runs round a room to chair height only, thereby protecting walls from furniture marks. This is less likely to consist of panels than of vertical tongued and grooved boards known as matchboards. These may have been renewed several times in the past, and as a present-day treatment they can do more for a room than mask faults in the lower parts of walls. Some people have revived with success an old practice of matchboarding the ceilings as well as walls.

Staircases provide stretches of wall space which can be used for hanging a series of prints—or even a valuable and decorative rug which you do not need elsewhere. It may be that the walls in your cottage, by reflecting your choice of pictures, books and other items kept on view, will give more meaning to the rooms than the cleverest, artiest colour scheme.

A fireplace occupies several square feet of a wall and,

though it may not be in use as a source of heat, it remains a visually important item in an old cottage. If you have removed castellated tilework to expose the original opening, you can equip it with andirons for logs and a fireback, or with a basket grate on legs. To avoid smoke in the room, raise the hearth on a layer or two of bricks.

A fire must have, from somewhere, a continuous supply of air to enable its flue to draw away the products of combustion. Movements of air towards the grate are particularly noticeable under a low ceiling. A screen can give protection, but a lasting remedy is to provide the fireplace with its own local air supply, a job which is easy where the floor is hollow. Several holes of pencil thickness should be drilled on either side of the hearth, or two large holes cut and fitted with gratings approximately 9in by 6in. As soon as the fire is burning, air will be drawn to exactly the point where it is needed.

With a solid floor, it would be necessary to excavate and put in a duct, consisting of a tube, leading to an outside wall; two tubes would help to counter-balance variations in wind pressure. One drawback to guard against is the entry of wildlife. Along with the rush of air through the first duct I made came a field mouse.

Late Georgian and early nineteenth-century grates of the hob type are especially desirable in a cottage sitting-room. These were some of the first grates to be fitted tightly to each side of the fireplace instead of standing free in the middle. They were usually cast iron (but with fire bars of wrought iron) and had relief decoration on the side panels. They are no longer commonly seen in cottages, long years of use having worn them out. But the genuine article, taken from the bedrooms of big houses, can still be bought or found; it could be that such an article would be exactly right for your room.

Walls, grates and shelves

Round, Georgian-type tripod table, easy to place. With three legs instead of four a table stands firm on an uneven cottage floor

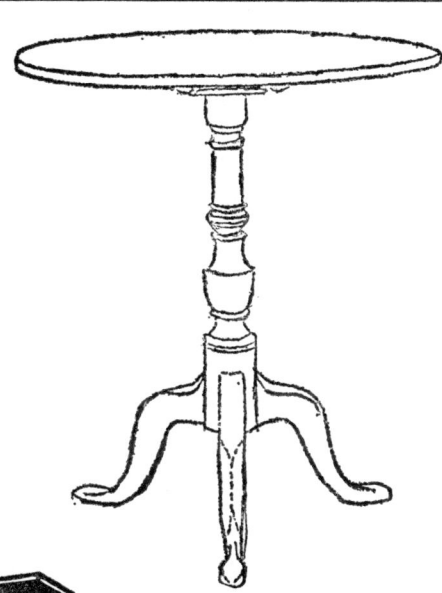

Bureau bookcase of simplified Chippendale design. A useful piece which agreeably dominates any room

Walls, grates and shelves

Where no unfortunate alterations have been carried out, look twice at existing built-in fireplaces: you may be the owner of a grimy Victorian grate, ripe for cleaning up, which could once again lend quiet dignity to the room. The standard designs for casting nineteenth-century grates were the result of deep thought; some are most attractive. The kind tight-fitted from about 1845 and made of ornamented cast iron are often well worth keeping. They are much sought after as antiques.

Mid-Victorian parlour grate of a kind worth keeping

You should also examine any existing old surround to a fireplace and imagine it with its coats of black or dark brown paint transformed by gloss white to match the rest of the room. These surrounds—generally of wood or cast iron—were often charming in their proportions and simple design. Several London shops stock reproductions in wood and also make them to order.

Shelves lined with books or china look extremely well against white walls. They can be made to cover an entire wall, from floor to ceiling, and are as suitable in other parts of the cottage as in the sitting room. Painting the shelves white will make them demonstrably part of the architecture of the room, leaving the books to provide colour and contrast; but there is also much to be said for the warm effect of the natural shade of unpainted wood against a light wall.

It used to be the practice in cottages for cupboards with a broad counter at waist level to be built into the recesses on each side of a chimney breast. If your cottage has these cupboards, the space above could be filled up to the ceiling with bookshelves. A wall facing a window provides a setting for a large spread of bookshelves, which may nicely balance the room.

Unless you already have a collection of books, it is worth bearing in mind that you can pick them up in lots quite cheaply at auction salerooms, second-hand junk shops and market stalls, and even local jumble sales. Such purchases could be derided as demoting books to the status of wallpaper bought by the yard, but very often the results are rewarding and something of real interest turns up. And what pleasanter use could be made of a country cottage than to sit back beside a blazing log fire and dip into books? Plenty of people admit that the course of their lives, or the direction of their interests, has been changed as a result of reading a book which came to hand by chance.

CHAPTER 5

The kitchen

The kitchen is for most people the first room to put in working order, and then a bedroom, for with these two rooms equipped a cottage can be lived in without discomfort while being fitted and furnished.

If your cottage is vernacular and unsymmetrical in design, perhaps a small seventeenth-century farmhouse, the room that was the kitchen will be bigger than any other. It was allowed extra width because of the varied activities it was used for. An impressive feature of numerous old kitchens is the great bread oven of brick or stone. From around 1800 an oven was often built into existing cottages and included in new ones; before that date few cottagers had been able to afford to bake bread. A usual site is beside the fireplace, the door opening into the room, though sometimes into the actual hearth.

You may like to try baking bread in one of these ovens, which are surprisingly deep. The procedure is to stuff the oven full of twigs bound together, set fire to them and let them flare away until the oven gets suitably hot. For a thermometer all you need is a fire brick placed at the inner

The kitchen

end: when this glows white-hot, rake out the ashes and quickly put in the lumps of dough.

If you decide to go on using the original kitchen for cooking, you could make it an attractive warm room with space enough for having meals in comfort. It would be in fact an up-to-date version of the all-purpose room which the cottage kitchen used to be. But very often it is more convenient to fit modern kitchen units in a small scullery-washroom alongside (traditional home of a great stone sink, to be put outside for a bird bath) and thereby gain a dining room and, perhaps, a degree of privacy while cooking.

In the original kitchen you may have space for all the fittings that make life easier and also for plenty of wooden furniture: an old dresser, say, and a table and chairs of traditional design. The latter, you would find, set the style of the room, not the modern clean-lined, close-fitting pieces of equipment, the best of which are agreeably unobtrusive.

It often seems a good idea to keep an existing floor of brick or flagstones, but I suggest that such a floor could be troublesome to live with unless in excellent condition, and that carefully laid composition tiles—possibly black and white—would fit in well and be more comfortable to the feet. However, a cool stone-floored larder could be a blessing, even taking the place of a refrigerator.

To minimise work in a kitchen of any size—and accidents—the fittings should be grouped as compactly as possible. No doubt you have already decided where these should go and have introduced the necessary pipes, wiring and drains. If not, plan it out by drawing on the floor and walls with a pencil before any work is done.

Decide first on a place for the sink—that is to say, a modern sink unit with a stainless steel drainer, a cutlery drawer and cupboard space for pots and pans. This norm-

The Kitchen

ally goes best before the window with the taps just below the sill. Apart from giving a good light, the window offers something to look at as you do a routine job of cleaning or scraping. Some people are pleased if this window gives on to a village street, because they know that something of interest may happen at any moment—and it is obviously to the good if it can face south.

If possible, arrange the rest of the kitchen pieces so that when linked with a wide shelf, or 'working surface', they and the sink unit form an unbroken line. If it's a line with a right-angled bend in it, walking about is reduced to the minimum. A good place for a refrigerator is under the shelf linking sink and cooker.

An easily-installed electric cooker is most people's choice in a cottage, but where mains gas is laid on, as it could be in a village, you may be glad to harness it for cooking. Even in a remote cottage you could, if you liked, have gas piped to a cooker from your own cylinders, thereby securing an alternative source of heat which you would value in the event of an electricity failure. There might be a supplier in the district who would see to it that you never ran short. You would need two cylinders for safety; and by keeping these outside the cottage—it would need an Arctic temperature to freeze the gas—you would not have to be present when an empty one was replaced.

If you are to cook with one of the handsome modern versions of the old kitchen range, which would heat your water tank, you will probably have to install it in an existing fireplace cavity, as a flue will be needed. Large gaps between the cooker and the enclosing walls could usefully hold things like fuel containers and trays, but inaccessible slits collect grime and should be solidly filled in.

The drawback to cooking within a fireplace can be that there is no adjacent surface on which to stand things and

The kitchen

do pouring operations. And it may so happen that the doorway lies just between the cooker and the sink, an arrangement which could lead to an accident if a child hurried into the room as a pan of scalding liquid was being moved across.

Unexpected ideas for improving a kitchen often present themselves after you have begun to cook in it; where they involve structural work, it is as well to carry them out before too many delicate furnishings have been brought into the cottage. You may decide that the way the doors open could be improved. In a very small kitchen it may be found that standing and working space can be almost doubled by making one of the doors swing the opposite way or replacing it with a sliding door.

Is the electric light exactly where you want it? A place where a wall bracket is always welcome is just to one side of the window, illuminating both cooking and washing-up activities. A central lamp on a low ceiling tends, when you are working, to illuminate the upper part of your back rather than what is going on under your hands. Although wall lamps are troublesome to fit, as the flex should be chased in the plaster, they are economical as well as efficient in a kitchen, for each can have a bulb of medium wattage to give light just where it is needed.

Power points should be thoughtfully placed for plugging in your kettle, toaster, mixer or iron. The point for the kettle should obviously be near the taps, with a surface beside it for making hot drinks and a cupboard or shelf above for holding jars of tea, coffee and other beverages. A whole row of elevated cupboards with sliding doors, set above your kitchen units, would be invaluable for storing tinned and bottled foodstuffs.

I like oak or pine furniture in an old kitchen. Oak made almost white by constant scouring was once the pride

Windsor chairs for a kitchen: *(above)* eighteenth-century designs; *(below)* nineteenth-century designs. It has been suggested of these lively country chairs—by Barbara Jones—that if attacked with an axe they would fight back instead of disintegrating into planks and sticks

of the industrious cottage wife; for the less industrious a light protective film of polish gives an equally good effect. The dresser, sometimes painted, was considered an essential part of every rural kitchen from at least the mid-seventeenth century. It had a wide shelf for dressing food, with deep drawers and places for pots underneath and shelves above where all the household crockery was displayed. Some dressers were semi-fixtures, anchored to a stout fillet fixed to the wall and without any wooden backing to the shelves. Dressers are much in demand today; they can sometimes be found in shops which specialise in buying up old pieces, stripping them down and restoring them.

Windsor chairs are a pleasure to have in a cottage kitchen. These are the ones, always associated with High Wycombe in Buckinghamshire, with a saddle-shaped seat into which are fitted the legs and the back. The early handmade product was generally composed of a mixture of woods, with elm for the seat, beech or a fruitwood for the legs, and ash for the outer rail of the back. The chair back was given its horseshoe shape by means of a steaming and heating process.

High prices are asked today for the earlier Windsor chairs. The modern ones are equally comfortable and almost as resilient, elegant and lively in appearance; they can hardly be called reproductions, as the type has been made continuously in England since at least the first years of the eighteenth century. The carved centre splat, often incorporating a wheel, has been a common feature on this masterly chair for about 150 years.

There is a wide choice of other chairs of simple and attractive design: rush-seated spindlebacks and ladderbacks, and their modern versions which are little changed. William Morris, famous for his wallpapers, is to be

Furniture for cottage kitchens illustrated in J. C. Loudon's *Cottage, Farm and Villa Architecture*, 1833: *(above)* a typical dresser is here supplied with rails so that plates lean outwards and are protected from dust; *(below)* light chairs of a kind still often seen

The kitchen

remembered almost as much for the rush-seated chair manufactured and made popular by his firm; it was not his own invention, but copied with trifling improvements from a chair made in a Sussex village.

Page 51 Sitting room, with bookshelves fitted into recess formed by chimney breast; log basket, tripod table, modern wing chair

Page 52 Dining room: *(above)* inglenook showing where bread oven formerly opened into hearth; Norfolk-latched door on left led to stairs. In foreground, refectory table; *(below)* another view of same room, with corner shelves, drawered side table and hoop-back Windsor chairs

CHAPTER 6

Bedrooms

Furnishing the bedrooms of an old cottage often calls for ingenuity. Indeed, it may seem impossible at first to get more than pillows and blankets up the narrow twisting staircase. The early cottagers, going to bed by the sun, may have had a built-in cupboard or two, but they brought little furniture upstairs. Sometimes their only means of reaching the upper floor was by a ladder.

People have been known to take out window frames and knock down walls to get a piece of furniture into a bedroom. If you have to consider this, make as certain as you can that the article is going to look right when it is in place: measuring and making sketches can help. Once I recklessly divided a seventeenth-century oak press cupboard into two sections by sawing it down the middle, only to realise when it was put together again with battens and screws that it swamped the attic room it stood in. I sent it, partially ruined, to an auction saleroom.

Cottage bedrooms are often situated well up under the roof. The awkward wedge-shaped space formed by a sloping ceiling can be filled by built-in cupboards, some with

Bedrooms

hanging space, others with shelves or drawers. The conventional wardrobe, if it has somehow been squeezed into a cottage bedroom, can appear almost menacing.

Where the room has a chimney breast, an excellent place for built-in cupboards and shelves is the recess on either side. The cupboard frame should extend from floor to ceiling, taking in an upper section for the storage of blankets or suitcases. Separate upper doors are unlikely to be necessary in a low-ceilinged room.

To allow for the width of a loaded coathanger, the depth of a hanging cupboard should not be less than 22in, which is a few inches more than the average depth of a chimney-breast recess. For easy cleaning, the cupboard floor should be an unrestricted continuation of the rest of the floor. The cupboard doors can either be plain, and papered or painted to match the walls, or made to match the style of the bedroom door.

Even the smallest bedroom in an old cottage may have a fireplace. It should not necessarily be done away with, because, as well as offering the occasional pleasure of a flickering fire, it acts—when the flue is open—permanently and efficiently as a ventilator. The grate recess makes a safe place for an electric radiant heater. However, I should say at this point that for maximum safety, particularly in a child's room, it is better to have an electric blower or convector heater; or, where there is no electricity, a calor gas heater of the no-flame catalytic type.

In some bedrooms, a fireplace may be considered a waste of wall space. If so, you can seal off the flue and fit a whitewood chest of drawers into the opening, flush with the surrounding wall.

The decoration of a bedroom depends not only on individual taste, but on its size, shape, the presence of beams and the position of doors and windows. Wallpaper of an appropriate pattern can give colour to an otherwise featureless or dimly-lit room. If plain walls seem preferable, as they may in a restricted space, then existing paper can be painted over.

Bedroom-quality carpet is inexpensive, being made to withstand less wear. Close-fitted, it adds considerably to the comfort of an upstairs room. An individual carpet, within a surround; haircord or matting; rugs on polished boards —all may be suitable to a particular room.

The principal item of furniture is obviously the bed. If possible, choose one with legs that unscrew; while rigid ones can be sawn off to negotiate a staircase, it is not a simple job to re-attach them securely. A modern double bed, with the whole frame hinged down the middle, is often easier to install than a single. The old-fashioned bedstead with built-in head and foot boards can be bought secondhand and made very comfortable with a new or renovated base; reproduction beds of this type are also procurable. The plain, hospital-style metal bed, easily manoeuvrable when dismantled, can be attractively painted to suit the decor of a cottage bedroom.

Modern coil-spring divans have a choice of head boards, in several materials and colours, which can be slotted into the base. Secondhand beds bought at an auction sale for a few pounds are often found to have become too soft. Even brand-new divans, in the cheaper price bracket, have this same fault: lack of firm support, which can cause worse backache than sleeping on the floor.

Where a bed is to be slept on regularly, it is worth paying extra for good quality springs. If you possess a horse-hair mattress in good condition, many people would envy you; these give excellent support on a box-spring base, but are now only made to order.

Bed sizes went metric in 1971, and although the familiar

Bedrooms

2ft 6in, 3ft and 4ft 6in sizes are still available, these are now called small sizes. The new standard size are 90cm (2ft 11½in), 100cm (3ft 3in) and 200cm (4ft 11½in). They are longer as well as wider. Ideally a bed should be at least 6in longer than the person sleeping on it. The new metric sizes may call for bigger sheets and blankets.

Low divans are specially suitable in bedrooms with limited headroom. By placing such a bed beneath a sloping ceiling and fixing above it a valance and curtains, you can give it a four-poster effect. When deciding on the position for a bed, it is usually preferable not to have it opposite the window where you will directly face the daylight and be unable to read easily. If the bed is sideways to the window you are not bothered by glare and can still look outside.

The bedspread covers a large area in any cottage bedroom and for that reason a safe choice would be near-white or neutral. Floral material, perhaps identical with the curtains, works only if the design is fairly muted. A homemade patchwork quilt of many colours can be nevertheless a stunning success in a cottage room, especially if the walls are white. An alternative would be a peasant-style bedspread from Italy or Spain.

Bedside tables should be level with the mattress, at which height a cup of tea is within easy reach. A drawer beneath the table top can be convenient for small objects that create clutter, and a shelf below is welcome for books. A small writing table will certainly not go unused.

If anything in the room is to be an antique, let it be the chest of drawers. Not only aesthetically pleasing, it will do double duty as a dressing-table. Chests of drawers often get stuck on the way upstairs, demonstrating the value of the kind made in two sections. A chest of rather ordinary quality could reasonably be sawn across, but re-assembly

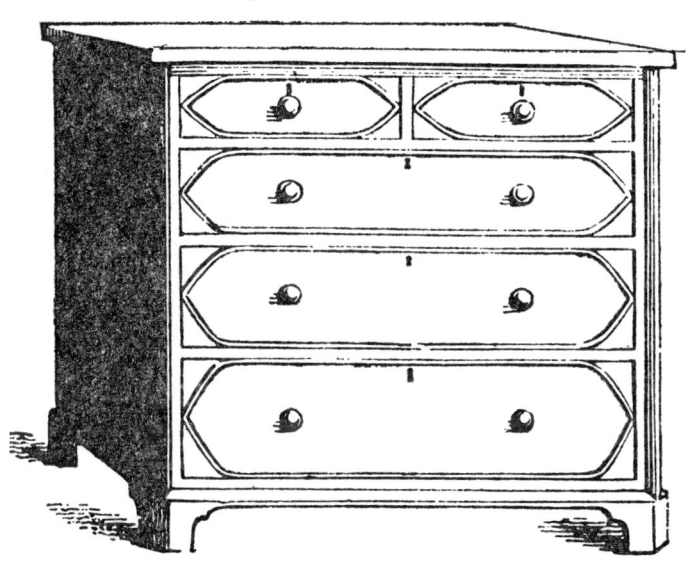

Chest of drawers for a cottager, early nineteenth century

would need careful work.

Check the handles of an old piece: there may be eight of them and they will be very noticeable. It is extraordinary how much handle-changing has gone on since around the middle of the nineteenth century, leaving its mark on the inside—and sometimes the outside—of the drawers. It is not difficult to get replacements suitable for the age and style of a particular chest. Beardmores of 4, Percy Street, London W1 keep an enormous stock of handles of every known pattern. Antique mahogany chests of drawers which are small are becoming very expensive but, having acquired one, you can reflect that its value will only increase while it usefully serves you.

There are plenty of Victorian and Edwardian chests of drawers—and new ones, too—which, if not too large, are suitable for cottages. Those made of deal, formerly com-

Bedrooms

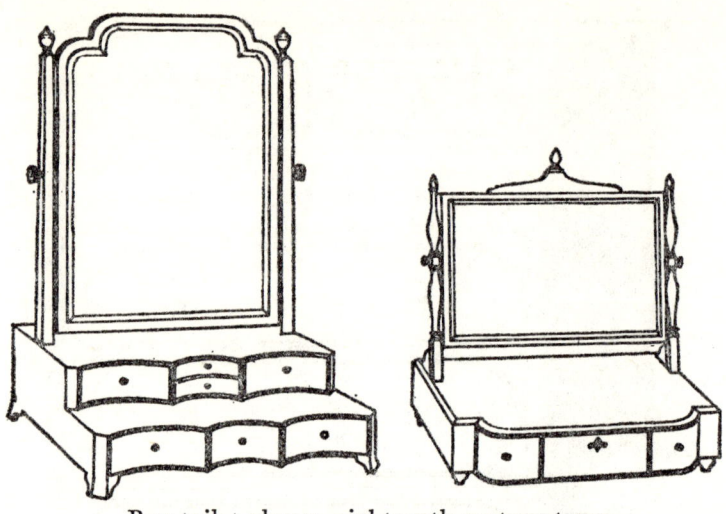

Box toilet glasses, eighteenth-century types

mon in servants' rooms, can be repainted, or stripped down and simply polished with wax. Military chests, old or new, fit well into cottage rooms because they are made in two sections, each containing two or more drawers. A nineteenth-century invention, the military chest was made of mahogany or cedar with sunk drawer handles of brass for easy stacking during transport, and usually similar handles at the ends for carrying. An old oak linen chest is another article which may suit a bedroom if not too large. With scattered cushions it could be useful to sit on as well as for storing sheets, blankets and eiderdowns.

Victorian pieces continue to be fashionable; even the marble-topped washstand, with its complementary jug and basin, is back in favour and may be just what is needed in a room where running water is not laid on. A small button-back chair or low rocking chair would look inviting beside a bedroom window. Plain wooden chairs, picked up cheap at sales, can be transformed by a coat of paint for use in attic bedrooms.

The position of windows will be a consideration in deciding where to put the main looking-glass. The obvious place for a hanging mirror is above a side table, while the free-standing box type functions well on top of a chest of drawers. A full-length mirror is always an asset and might be attached to the inside of a clothes cupboard door.

Lamps should be carefully placed to add to the convenience of a room. For reading in bed, either by a bedside-table lamp or an overhead wall fixture, the best height for the bulb is about 18in above the mattress. A coloured shade should be white inside to help illumination. You will need another lamp near the looking-glass—and it might be a good idea to see that this is the one which can be switched on and off at the door.

Given adequate heating, children's bedrooms can be designed for use also as daytime playrooms or places to study or carry on hobbies. Great advances have been made since the war in the design and quality of such items as the bunk bed, one example of which has a strong framework of beechwood and two easy-running drawers underneath the lower of the two beds. The structure can be divided into two free-standing adult-sized beds with head and foot boards. Bunk beds can wonderfully help you to squeeze two children and their belongings into a tight attic room. But make sure the structure is robust—especially the upper side rails—that the ladder hooks on properly and the devices for locking the beds together are proof against high-spirited treatment.

As an item of traditional country furniture, a mule chest would go well in a child's room: this is a lidded chest of modest proportions having a drawer, or two drawers, in the lower third. Strong old specimens, usually of

Bedrooms

oak or pine, turn up from time to time at provincial auction sales. A mule chest provides a child with a workbench or seat of convenient height as well as a place for toys at the top and clothes at the bottom. The term mule has the sense of hybrid, meaning that the piece has the characteristics of both a chest and a chest of drawers. A boy who is good at carpentry might set about making a mule chest for himself.

Whether an attic is to be used as a bedroom or as a playroom, it is worth taking advantage of today's direct-from-the-factory furniture, which is delivered in sections, ready to be assembled in the room it is meant for.

CHAPTER 7

The sitting room

The sitting room is generally the most important room socially even if you have a cheerful kitchen in which neighbours can be entertained to coffee or home-made wine. It may take time to get the room exactly right; sometimes the best arrangement of furniture and pictures suggests itself only after years of occupation.

Before you begin furnishing, make sure there is nothing basically wrong. If you have a large picture window, a metal-framed window or the type with an upper section opening upwards and outwards, you might prefer to replace it with a wooden-barred window more in keeping with the period of the cottage. Don't be afraid to reduce the size of the opening. The outside of the cottage could be much improved by such an alteration and inside you would feel much more at ease: cottagers of the past well knew that small windows give both warmth and a sense of security.

Perhaps you have a new panelled door in the room. What kind of architrave has the door frame? Should there be mouldings for this and round the panels? If the mould-

The sitting room

ings are modern, you might want to change them to match others already existing in the cottage. Door mouldings have no place, though, in a really old cottage and are not suitable for ledged and braced doors.

The mouldings used for cottages in Georgian and Victorian times were chosen from a limited selection of standard types: nearly all of these are still procurable ready-made in joinery shops. They handsomely complete a job when used consistently; but they must also serve a purpose by covering over the joint, where shrinkage occurs, between the frame and panels or between the frame and enclosing plasterwork. Mouldings glued for effect to the entirely flat surface of, say, a cupboard door present a tiresome sham and deserve to be chipped off. If the room has a strip of moulding acting as a picture rail, this, too, would be best removed.

In an eighteenth- or nineteenth-century cottage, the sitting room is certain to be tiny unless it has been merged with another room or a passage: a standard size for parlours in the smaller Georgian houses was only 12ft by 12ft. However, a cottage dating from the seventeenth century or earlier may yield a good-sized room with enough primitive structural features in timber to offer what an architect might call a ready-made decorative scheme.

With a box-like room there is at least the possibility of raising the temperature from ice cold to warm in a few minutes; and feelings of confinement can be reduced by having a glass-paned door opening on to the garden or yard.

The sitting room almost certainly has a fireplace with recesses for built-in shelves, ideal for diplaying books and ornaments. In a cottage there is no need to have casing for shelves; simply rest them on battens attached to the enclosing walls; a wide shelf low down on one side of the fireplace could conveniently hold a television set.

The sitting room

Perhaps a fireplace has been blocked up, leaving a blank protruding chimney breast. Here you could take advantage of the disused flue behind and have a small but deep cupboard built in, where bottles and glasses could be kept. A good position for such a cupboard might be about 4ft from the floor, with its door flush with the wall and painted the same colour. Screw a picture or a mirror to the door, covering it entirely, and your cupboard would be completely concealed. A side table could then be placed underneath, against the lower part of the chimney breast.

One idea leads to another. You may think of other places in the room where it would be pleasant to have cupboards, shelves or drawers built in. In carrying out such work, in what is likely to be the warmest room in the cottage, it is worth bearing in mind that joinery in new softwood has a way of twisting and warping: all too often the wood has not been properly seasoned. Faults are especially liable to occur—within a month or so—in the doors of large cupboards where there is warm air on one side and colder, moister air on the other.

One foolproof way of avoiding warped doors, which are unsightly, inefficient and irreparable, is to use secondhand wood well past the stage of growing pains. At auction sales and junk shops, ugly and uselessly large wardrobes can be picked up and treated as a stock of fully seasoned wood which will not let you down. Another source of such wood is the demolition contractors, whose names and addresses may be found in classified telephone directories. In their yards, or at places where they are working, you should be able to buy good handmade doors for about 50p each and any amount of sound joists and floor boards. Be on the alert, though, for an excessive number of woodworm holes and for dry rot. Wood affected by dry rot is spongy, smells of mushrooms and has cracks going against the grain. The

The sitting room

blade of a knife, you will find, sinks straight in.

Usually it is necessary to make up your mind about the arrangement of the sitting-room furniture before settling on the position of the lights; but if you find at a late stage that you have made a mistake, don't let the mess that goes with re-chasing into plaster deter you from putting it right.

In a cottage it would be over-sophisticated to have concealed illumination or small, cleverly placed spotlights; and tubular strip lighting, praised for casting no shadows, seems hardly suitable either. Wall lamps fixed about a third of the way up give soft background light and can improve the look of the walls. There could be wall lights on either side of the window, perhaps, or flanking a group of pictures. When clip-on shades are to be fitted to a wall-lamp, the bulb should not be more than 60 watts: the extra heat of a 100-watt bulb would both scorch the shade and make a brown spot on the ceiling. Many bracket fittings on the market incorporate make-believe candle stumps complete with drips of wax. Well shaded, these can be acceptable; but I prefer simple swan-neck fittings in brass.

As an alternative to wall lighting, you may prefer table lamps and even one or two space-consuming standard lamps. The thing to avoid is the glare of an overhead light coming from one point in the middle of the ceiling. Install power points at several strategic positions in the room.

Now comes the laying of carpets and the hanging of curtains. If you are still undecided as to your choice of colour and pattern, take the easy way out and don't have too much of either in your background furnishings but bring them in casually in the form of accessories.

The harmonious or non-contrasting colours are the ones near each other in the prismatic order, shades of orange and yellow-orange being one example and shades of green and blue-green another (see the colour-wheel illustration,

The sitting room

page 67). There could be no crude clash if harmonious colours only were used, though the result would be rather dull. A room is much improved by the addition of a certain amount of complementary or contrasting colour such as red and green, orange and blue, which, as you will see, are opposite one another on the colour wheel. It is important to avoid having two large areas of more or less equal extent in contrasting colours, especially if neither is muted. A bright red sofa and easy chairs on a brilliant green carpet would be uncomfortable to look at. On the other hand, a small amount of red to complement a dominant green, or a splash of clear blue in a brown-orange room, would have a good effect. Most people achieve the desired result without conscious thought by introducing pictures, cushions, upholstery or curtains which contain the appropriate complementary colour. Herein lies one of the virtues of ornaments and bowls of flowers. The reason why wooden chairs are seen to advantage on a green carpet is illustrated by the fact that the colour of wood comes roughly opposite green on the colour wheel.

Floral upholstery or covers can look very well in a cottage sitting room and so can flower-patterned curtains, but to have both is often a mistake. In fact patterns of any kind are difficult to have together unless they are totally different. One solution might be to have patterned loose covers and plain yellow-ish, almost neutral curtains.

Once the room is equipped with joinery, a carpet and curtains, it begins to seem almost finished; and indeed little remains to make it habitable. Tables of various kinds will be needed and plenty of comfortable furniture to sit on. A lack of other things will be shown up quickly enough by occupation.

An old round-topped table can be a great asset in a cottage sitting room. I am thinking of the Georgian type,

The sitting room

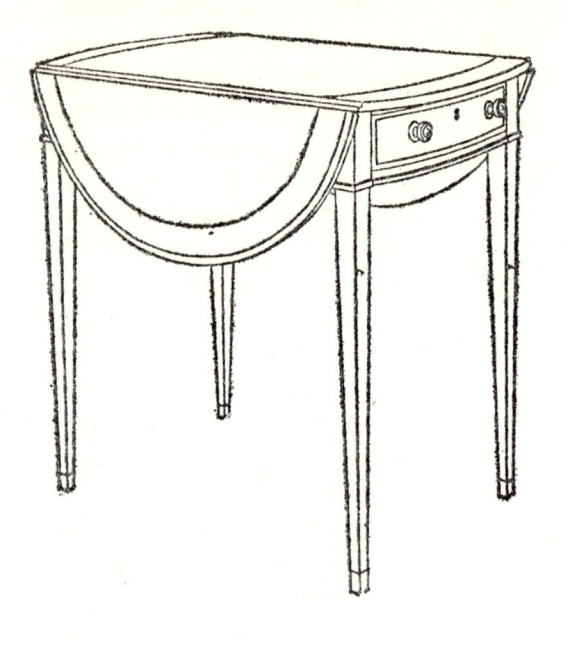

Tables for a sitting room: *(left)* Pembroke with drawer at one end and dummy drawer at other end; *(below, left)* space-saving Sutherland; *(below, right)* cricket table whose three legs give stability on uneven floors

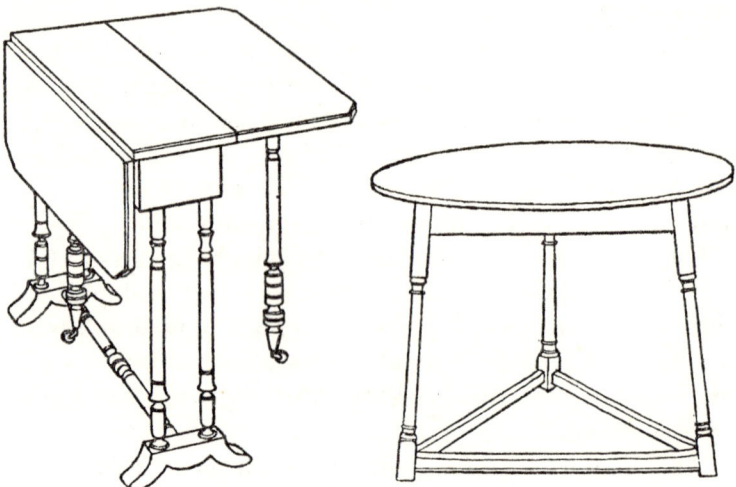

The sitting room

usually collapsible, with a turned pillar into which three cabriole legs are dovetailed. It would be worth looking about in antique shops and studying local auctioneers' catalogues in order to acquire one. The really valuable examples have ball-and-claw feet and pie-crusting, but the nice thing about furnishing a cottage is that pieces with such refinements are not wanted. Even today, the prices of eighteenth-century, country-made furniture can sometimes compare favourably with those of their brand new reproductions.

Some of the smaller Victorian pieces, such as sewing tables, little Davenport desks and inlaid papier mâché chairs, might fit into your sitting room admirably. Regency sable-legged chairs and convex mirrors often look too showy in a cottage setting of uneven plaster-work, beams and stone floors. Even when new, Regency furniture in country dwel-

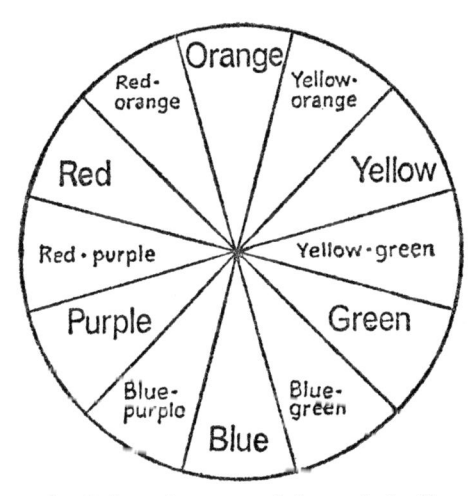

The colour wheel, based on a rainbow, is built up from the primary colours red, yellow and blue and the secondary colours orange, green and purple

The sitting room

lings drew adverse comments from William Cobbett: he saw a selection in an ancient farmhouse and in *Rural Rides*, 1825, wrote of 'the mahogany table and the fine chairs and the fine glass, and all as barefaced upstart as any stockjobber in the kingdom can boast of'.

It may be that you own some quite large pieces and are anxious somehow to find a place for them. A grand piano will only find a niche where several rooms have been knocked into one large sitting room; but an antique secretaire bookcase, apart from being useful, would look most decorative between two windows or against the wall opposite the fireplace. If the room is rectangular, it could be placed against one of the longer walls to retain and accentuate the sense of space given by the length of the room. Beware of standing a rectangular piece of furniture—even a long-case clock—across a corner: almost invariably this looks uneasy as well as blocking off dead triangular space.

Perhaps you have an old bureau or a card table. Both should settle in well. The desk should obviously have access to daylight for writing; and it might be ideally accompanied by a spindle-back chair or a country Chippendale with lift-out seat of woolwork.

Despite the fact that it is of more recent date, seat furniture which is fatly sprung and padded goes well in

American cottage furniture of mid-nineteenth century

the sitting room of an old cottage. A sofa of some kind is particularly desirable and none is more suitable than a Chesterfield, which has arms and back of the same height. This is a Victorian design of about 1880; versions of it, especially smaller ones, have been made ever since, but those of today are absurdly expensive.

It was the mid-Victorians who first allowed comfortable layers of upholstery to determine the shape of seat furniture. All that padding makes a floor-consuming lump, however, in a small room. If there are to be easy chairs as well as a sofa, let them be on a smaller scale, and not *en suite*. Winged armchairs, easily bought secondhand or in reproduction, are comfortable and draught-absorbing. To give full satisfaction a chair must support the small of the back and be large enough to let you change position easily.

A three-piece suite, however handsome, may have to be split up for lack of space or to avoid swamping a small sitting room. If it is to be fitted in, however, consider covering the sofa in a material that is markedly lighter in colour than that covering the chairs, thereby reducing any oppressive effect.

Water-colours and old prints look well with thin black or gold frames, or thick ones of maplewood. A large stretch of featureless wall could serve as a setting for pictures of various sizes arranged in clusters. Spread them out first on the floor to see how they will look. Such an arrangement is shown off best if it forms a group with something else, such as a piece of furniture beneath; and, if one picture is to go above another, the upper picture should be the bigger. Don't knock nails right home until you are fairly sure a picture is in the right place. Hang with picture wire rather than string or cord, which eventually weaken. When you are entirely happy with the siting of a picture—perhaps after some weeks of living with it—it can be clamped un-

The sitting room

obtrusively to the wall by means of pierced brass plates and screws. This will prevent it from being accidentally knocked from the wall or just made crooked in the course of dusting.

A mirror with a thick gilded frame can be a most pleasant part of the furnishings of a cottage sitting room. Antique mirrors lose their value if murky, raw-silvered glass is replaced by new. Secure fixing to the wall is obviously essential. The time-honoured position is above the mantlepiece, where it should be large enough to balance the fireplace opening, but wherever you have it you will notice that, like a pond in a garden, it will give to the room a bit of extra life.

CHAPTER 8

The dining room

Small dining rooms in the country which linger pleasantly in the memory are often, you may agree, low-ceilinged, short of daylight, rather cool in summer, illuminated by the flames of an open fire and candles in winter, and smelling faintly at all times of wood ash or pot-pourri. Although the dining room is a mid-eighteenth-century innovation for houses, such a room can be appointed to appear entirely in keeping with a cottage.

The main item of furniture is, of course, the table, which should have a distance between it and the walls of about 2ft 6in to allow for movement of chairs. Gateleg tables are attractive pieces which have been giving good service in country rooms since the middle of the seventeenth century. The early oak type with four central legs, and railed gates to support the flaps, provides less knee room than the Georgian type, often mahogany, which has gates modified to single legs swinging out from the central frame. Oval has always been the favourite shape for gate tables.

Another good-looking small table for a pocket-sized room is the Pembroke, a late eighteenth-century design associated

The dining room

with Sheraton, seating four people in comfort. Flaps hang on each of the longer sides and rest on fly brackets when opened up. There is usually a drawer, useful for cutlery, at one end of the central part and at the other end a matching dummy drawer. For slightly larger rooms, the type of table known as refectory can be appropriate.

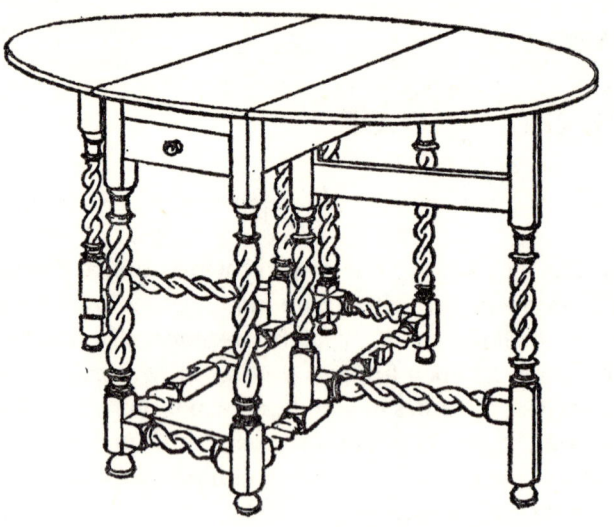

Table for a dining room: early gate leg

Modern versions of all these tables are being made today. Avoid buying the kind of Regency table with a pillar and a brass-footed tripod, of which many thousands have been reproduced; in most old cottages they tend to look a little pretentious.

When buying a new table, make sure it is of solid wood —too often the easily-worked chipboard is used for table tops and hidden by a thin veneer or by a wood-like film achieved photographically. Think twice, too, about those factory products which emerge spuriously rustic and hewn.

The dining room

Plenty of simply-designed and honestly-made tables are to be bought in the modern furniture shops. Round tops are good-looking on non-extending tables, especially in square rooms: needless to say a round room—as in a converted oasthouse—demands the relief of a square table.

Windsor chairs and rush- or cane-seated ladderbacks of all kinds are easily come by. Carved chairs of Chippendale type always look right with Georgian tables; the early, and rather heavy, country Chippendales are rare now, but so many Chippendale-type chairs were turned out at the end of the nineteenth century that acceptable versions are constantly on the market.

I would not myself be happy with the mixture of old chairs with which some people surround a cottage dining table. Chairs needn't be identical (sets tend to be extremely costly), but it is preferable, I suggest, to have them all of the same type and matching near enough. This can be quite easily and inexpensively achieved. You might be able in a single round of junk shops to collect, for example, three pairs of rush-seated country chairs, all of them a little different yet forming a group of chairs that are evidently related to one another. Judging by my own recent experience, an average price for each chair might be between £2 and £3.

There are always plenty of Victorian chairs to be picked up: little chairs with a top rail like a yoke, balloon-backs, and several varieties of pre-1914 bedroom chairs, with cane seats probably in need of repair.

Modern chairs of good design are easier to find today because of the competitive influence of Scandinavian and other imported products. Chairs of stick construction based on the Windsors can look most attractive; if you don't like the colour of the wood, there is precedent enough for painting them. Space-saving modern benches and stools, which

Chairs for a dining room: *(above)* spindle back and ladder back; *(below)* balloon back and Morris chair. These differ from the Windsors in being made by joiners rather than turners

can be fitted beneath the table when not in use, are often worth considering.

Modern sideboards, wherever you look, serve as a reminder that these pieces probably reached their only possible satisfactory shape on the drawing boards of designers like Adam, Hepplewhite and Sheraton. The ugliness of Victorian specimens with their fussy applied ornament, has

Modern versions of the Windsor chair and wing easy chair

merely been exchanged for a different kind of ugliness; nothing has emerged to equal the appeal of Georgian shapes.

If you can't find an old sideboard—some people like to use a Victorian chiffonier—you could acquire at considerable expense a faithful reproduction. However, this might look too smooth in a cottage room. A better idea would be to put in a dresser, removing the superstructure of shelves if you feel it makes the room look too much like a kitchen, or a plain side table with drawer. A built-in shelf with two

The dining room

drawers beneath it might be the answer; fixtures of this sort need not be offensive if they conform to the structure of the room. Whichever type of serving board you choose, a few pictures will add interest to the stretch of wall above, if there are no shelves.

The eighteenth-century dumbwaiter, a celebrated invention for dining rooms, is invariably out of place in a cottage. It may appear an attractive little tripod structure in the illustrations of furniture books; but in reality its height proves to be about 4ft 6in, and the three circular tiers revolving on a central shaft call for a lot of space. The dumbwaiter was designed for grand dining rooms; half a dozen, stacked with delicacies, would be disposed round the table at dessert time with the idea of allowing conversation to flow without the check imposed by the presence of servants. The modern square dumbwaiter on large wheels can be a useful rolling sideboard for a cottage where access to the kitchen is through a door with no step down or up.

Since the dining room, which is easy to keep neat, is likely to be the showpiece of the cottage, a little care is adviseable over the mixing of woods. Although different kinds can be mixed, you will notice that those which are markedly unlike in grain and tone do not look well together: for instance, teak chairs with a walnut table, and mahogany chairs with an oak table.

Oak with its rugged texture and weight rarely mixes well; it may look all right with other indigenous woods, such as elm and the fruitwoods (old Windsor chairs commonly contain four or five humble woods), but it will not be at ease alongside the fine reddish grain of mahogany or rosewood. It is not surprising that people starting with one oak piece feel that their choice must be between all oak or no oak at all.

It is often convenient to keep bottles and glasses in the

dining room. A corner cupboard, perhaps with glass doors, can prove ideal for the purpose, or for displaying china. In its hanging form, this is a piece of furniture with a long history, for it seems to have developed from a primitive fixture—shelves let into the plaster, or supported on battens, and enclosed by a door. The tall, freestanding corner cupboard dates only from the late seventeenth century. Particularly suitable as space-savers in cottage interiors, corner cupboards have maintained their popularity over the years, as is apparent from the large number still in existence.

It is probable that you have already supplied your dining room with electric light and power points, making sure that the table will be properly lit. Although usually avoided in other rooms, a lamp hanging from the ceiling is generally the best kind for the dining room. Arrange for it to hang quite low and be so shaded that it shines on the table rather than into the faces of the diners. You may not always want to dine by candlelight.

If your dining room was originally the kitchen living-room of a small seventeenth-century farmhouse, it is likely to retain signs of its former importance as the centre of all family activities. The fireplace may once have been a huge inglenook or chimney-corner allowing space for chairs round a log fire on the hearth. If a full unblocking operation has been done, you may have restored the fireplace to a state it last knew over a hundred and fifty years ago, because fireplaces were often reduced in size around the beginning of the nineteenth century. Coal was more plentiful and cooking in pots suspended over hearth fires was becoming old-fashioned. Hob grates were built into the fireplace—the space occupied by one of the hobs came to be used for a separate cast-iron oven and that occupied by the other for a boiler from which hot water could be ladled.

The dining room

Eventually there evolved the kitchen range, which contained these conveniences in one unit.

Old ranges are beginning to be valued as antiques, though perhaps not in a dining-room fireplace. Make use of a wide hearth by lighting a log fire on special occasions, set in a basket or andirons—with perhaps a fireback behind and a metal-mesh fire screen in front. The warmth, scent and flames add greatly to the friendly atmosphere of a dining room in use for entertaining.

CHAPTER 9

The bathroom

A suitable place for a bathroom can usually be found without building on or losing a whole room. If you visit other restored cottages, you may see a compact little bathroom formed from part of a bedroom or passage, or cunningly won, with the creation of a dormer window, from space in the roof. A converted coal shed, wash-house or larder, though inconveniently distant from bedrooms, is easier to plumb than somewhere upstairs and has the advantage that it can double as a cloakroom.

If finding space for a bathroom in a very small cottage presents an insuperable problem, then the answer is either to install a shower or make use of a tub. A Continental hip bath, which is on two levels so that you sit on a kind of step, is only 3ft 6in long and can be covered, taps and all, with a hinged lid. I once had one of these in the sitting room of my London flat and seldom thought of it as a bath except when I wanted to use it. Needless to say, most purchasers of old cottages, where there is piped-in water, will go to some lengths to acquire a bathroom.

The fitting-up of bathrooms has been the subject of an

The bathroom

almost unreasonable amount of attention in the last few years. Reports have been prepared for American universities; glossy magazines have published scores of articles and beguiling photographs; several full-length books have been written. The possibilities seem endless when you look through, for instance, the 1970 edition of Gontran Goulden's *Bathrooms*.

There is in theory no reason why the bathroom of a country cottage—a bathroom being a modern invention—should not be as luxurious and decorative as that of a metropolitan flat. I can only suggest that the comments of visitors could become a bore and that all anyone expects of a cottage bathroom is efficiency, hygiene and modest comfort. And you may agree with me, looking round, that coloured baths and basins are pointlessly showy compared with ordinary ones which, being white, appear to recede.

For efficiency, the room must offer enough space for the bather to go through the drying actions without obstruction from walls; the width should therefore be at least 6ft. It is nice to have a normal window, however small, in a bathroom; but remember that building regulations now allow artificial ventilation by means of an extractor fan. Perhaps, though, you can spare a room of reasonable size for your bathroom; if so it might be convenient to let it serve also as a dressing room, or as a laundry room that would keep the kitchen free of washing.

One of the least suitable wall treatments for bathrooms liable to be cold, and having poor insulation, is gloss paint; water will collect on it in ripples—more readily than on shiny paper—and drip on naked flesh from the ceiling.

Condensation is avoidable, certainly, by plenty of steady warmth, but this can be expensive. An electrically heated towel rail will provide steady warmth, but too little. In the absence of a central heating system, an efficient though

The bathroom

expensive radiator is the oil-filled kind worked by electricity. For short term use, an infra-red bar beams down its warmth in a most welcome manner, and is often well sited in the angle of wall and ceiling above the door. A paraffin stove quickly raises the temperature of the room, but does little for condensation since it produces water vapour itself as a product of combustion.

Whatever the space available, your bathroom should contain, as well as the bath (of enamelled cast iron or steel), a lavatory pan, a wash basin with shelf, a well-lit mirror, a heated towel rail, hooks for clothes, a cupboard, and something on the floor in addition to the bath mat which is comfortable to the feet. A cupboard for the lavatory brush and other cleaning materials is best built in beneath the basin, concealing the pipework there; it will look well made of tongued and grooved boards (matchboarding). Given enough space, there should also be a seat or stool and a linen basket.

I list the lavatory pan second only to the bath because nowadays most people appreciate the advantage of having it near means of washing; in the various recent publications I have looked at it is unanimously accepted as a bathroom object rather than something to go in a tapless little room on its own. This marks a sensible change in domestic thinking of recent years. In 1940 Mrs C. G. Tomrley stated in *Furnishing Your Home*: 'There is no doubt at all that a bathroom and wc in one is a second-rate arrangement, and if a house or flat offers you this, ten to one it is badly planned throughout'.

My list for a cottage bathroom includes no bidet: views may change, just as they have changed over the placing of WCs but this cold and naked-looking appliance, offering a convenience to be secured by other means, seems at present a poor joke in an English country cottage.

The bathroom

With the essential items in mind, work out on paper and by marking the walls, where they are all to go. The householder, knowing the needs of those who will use the room, can often do this as well as any architect. Sometimes the shape of the room will govern the position of the biggest item, the bath; if there is a sloping ceiling, for example, the only place may be hard underneath this.

When the things are being installed it is worth making sure the work does not create new draught inlets. This is liable to happen—with unsupervised workmen—where the room has timber-framed walls. Interior laths and plaster get broken away as the bath is fitted, the cavities are not made good and cold air is allowed to enter through chinks in the outer cladding of tiles or weather boards. Neat panelling round the bath is not enough to keep it back. There could also be draught inlets, concealed from sight, at the points where walls have been pierced to let out waste pipes.

A cheerful, warm-looking wallpaper is often appreciated in a cottage bathroom, though the wall round the bath should be protected by tiles. Bold wall patterns are best avoided, especially if the ceiling as well as the walls are to be papered. Papers which are not already waterproofed can be painted with a clear lacquer. If you decide against paper, you could not go wrong in having white, or pale pink walls, black panelling round the bath and a black lavatory seat and lid. Colour can be introduced by curtains, towels, bathmat and tooth mugs.

Because of the presence of water and danger of electric shocks, electrical appliances should be installed professionally. Either have cord pull switches or, safer still, arrange that it is only possible to switch anything on from outside the room. If you like to read in the bath and are having a central light as well as a light by the mirror, be careful not to fix it in such a position that you have to stand in the bath to change the bulb.

Floor covering and window draperies are usually tackled last on the list of bathroom works, the furniture of this room being screwed in position rather than moveable as elsewhere. Not the least of a floor covering's purposes is to form a barrier to draughts coming from between boards and under skirtings; it should be firmly secured and fit snugly up to the walls. Linoleum and cork have long been the traditional material, but both are inclined to be chilly and slippery when wet. A tiled surface may seem a good idea, but a carpet looks and feels much more comfortable.

About ten years ago people used to argue that carpets in the bathroom would rot, smell mouldy and generally give trouble. They have stood the test of time and have been found to give only pleasure. Provided the room has a means of heating, they dry rapidly after being splashed. So get as good a pile carpet as you wish, and don't forget a thick underfelt. An all-over neutral shade, or a pastel colour, would go well in a white bathroom. If there is a wallpaper it might be a good idea to choose a colour which picks up the predominant colour in the pattern.

Windows look cold without some kind of fabric accessory, and if they are very small they are sometimes best fitted with roller blinds. Frosted glass secures privacy, but so, much more attractively, do blinds or curtains which let in the light yet cannot be seen through. In general, have your bathroom curtains as cheerful as possible: pale yellow-orange ones give a pleasant idea of sunlight on a dull day.

There is one other bathroom article I haven't mentioned, and that is a medicine cupboard; to find wall space for this is not likely to be impossible. Where young

The bathroom

children are present, I do recommend the kind invented by Barry Bucknell as a safeguard against accidents to children: its door catch is inside a small round hole and can be easily reached by an adult's finger but not by a child's.

A downstairs cloakroom near the front door—and the garden—is a desirable amenity in any cottage. And it should contain a tap and basin so that visitors do not automatically make for the kitchen sink to wash their hands. There are some neat round basins to be had which fit in corners. A cloakroom need be scarcely larger than an under-stairs broom cupboard, a worse drawback than smallness being lack of a window. It is not convenient, or permissable, to form a cloakroom which leads without intervening lobby straight out of a living room.

Should you have a cloakroom of reasonable size, you could get away with cheerful overcrowding—and never mind the extra housework it will cause. You could festoon the walls with pictures and calendars hard to place elsewhere, put up a shelf for books and old magazines, use the place as a repository for gumboots and grubby raincoats, and let the dog sleep there. Make the room as warm and convenient as possible—wooden lavatory seats and lids are more comfortable than plastic ones which are invariably chilly and sometimes sharp-edged. Lavatory-paper holders are available in a variety of designs, but it may be preferable to have the roll loose on a handy ledge. In maintaining either a bathroom or a cloakroom, make sure that there is always soap, a towel, a mirror, a comb and a nailbrush. You would not like to think of visitors struggling to avoid asking for a missing item. Lighting need be no problem. In a tiny room one good light over the mirror —either on a bracket or hung from the ceiling—is all that is wanted.

Page 85 Fireplaces: *(right)* Millstone forms the hearth in a room formerly a miller's kitchen. Note the comfortable Chesterfield *(below)* A cast-iron hob grate. Neither fireplace calls for a surround

Page 86 Bedroom and bathroom:
(left) Hanging cupboards, which could have been extended to sloping ceiling, papered to match walls—and curtains
(below) similar all-over wallpaper treatment, though bath panel is of tongued and grooved boards

CHAPTER 10

The spare room

More accidents take place in kitchens than on the roads. We spend a third of our lives in bed. These are propositions fit for desultory discussion, but there is no arguing the proposition that a weekend visitor on average spends as many as eighteen hours in his bedroom.

Indeed, his time there could be longer, even twenty-four hours, if he lingers over the breakfast and papers you bring him. It can be amusing to put yourself in his place and anticipate his needs. The essential furnishings of a spare room are so few—a good bed, a lamp, curtains, a heater, a wall peg, a mirror and some books—that no cottage room can be too small to accommodate them.

The bed should be in particularly good order, with a proliferation of pillows and blankets, to be discarded or used according to personal inclination. Draping of the window is very important, especially if it faces east and therefore gets the sun from dawn onwards. You may yourself have had the experience, when away, of being woken by a brilliant shaft of sunlight at 6 am and having three sleepless hours to pass before breakfast; not everyone can

The spare room

bring himself to read a book at that time. Curtains should be lined and hung carefully, extending above the lintel and below the sill to exclude chinks of light. There is nothing against providing dark roller blinds as well. After all, the visitor who enjoys direct access to light and country air through an open window will simply leave the curtains undrawn.

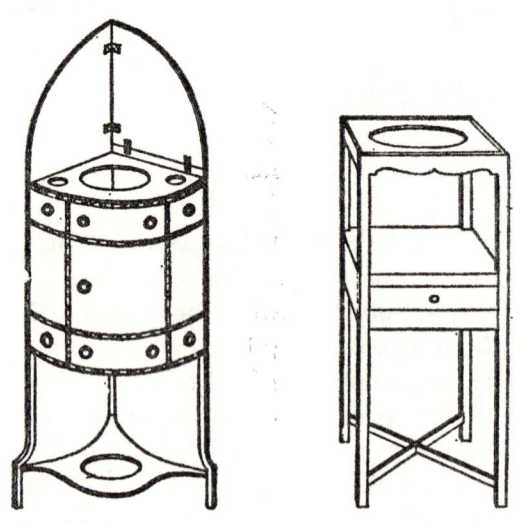

Washstands of late eighteenth-century type. Stand on the left has flaps which protect wall when raised and conceal basin hole when let down

In cramped quarters a perfectly good place to hang clothes is on the back of the door. Strong hooks and a clothes hanger are the only requirements. Given enough space, you would, of course, install a single chair with a top rail wide enough for a man's coat; also a bedside table, a writing table with paper and pens on it, a waste paper basket and possibly an upholstered armchair. There is normally no need for a chest of drawers; your weekend guest will not use it except to open the drawers in a spirit of friendly curiosity.

A mirror, seemingly obvious, can easily get forgotten in a newly prepared spare room; it is probably best attached to a wall in a good light or near a wash basin. If a basin is concealed in a walk-in cupboard—a very good place for it—be sure to mention the fact. If there is no running water in the room, why not install an antique or semi-antique washstand? The earlier ones, by no means hard to come by, are small and elegant; some even have a fully enclosed receptacle for dirty water. A late eighteenth-century type which is now rare and valuable has a mahogany-encased cistern with brass tap.

Clearly a washing place of any kind should be supported by towels, soap, a carafe of drinking water and a glass, but you could improve on this by unobtrusively adding a bottle of aspirins, a pair of nail scissors, a comb, a bottle of disinfectant and a tin of adhesive plasters. A vase of flowers would be appreciated on arrival, but avoid too many ornamental items of china or glass which would be a source of embarrassment if broken.

Any article capable of causing a fire should be operated as far as possible by you. When heating the spare room with an oil stove, light it yourself and remove it before your visitor goes to bed. If candles are used, the most suitable candlesticks are the brass or pewter type with a low socket mounted on a saucer and having a carrying handle. These chamber candlesticks, which used to be in ordinary everyday use for carrying upstairs to bed, were known throughout much of the nineteenth century as flat candlesticks or simply flat candles. Some had small clip-on extinguishers in the form of a cone.

If you have electricity, a closed-in electric heater is safe enough, though the open kind, glowing red, which may

The spare room

seem a more cheerful source of warmth, should be safely put out of the way inside a fireplace or otherwise protected. The controls are best beside the bed, enabling your visitor to switch off, and on again in the morning, without getting out of bed.

Make sure that everything works: bulbs don't last indefinitely, and the electric blanket should be checked for faulty elements. Light switches should be so placed that a stranger to the cottage can easily find them in the dark. For use during power failures, keep an electric torch in the room; perhaps a candle and matches, too.

Unless there is space for a bookshelf or two, an assortment of reading matter can be assembled between bookends, probably on the windowsill. Edited diaries, works on the flora and fauna of the district, collections of essays or sermons, are often relegated to the spare room. It doesn't at all matter if they are dull: starting to read a really dry book soon makes a person in a strange bed feel drowsy where an exciting, well written novel can have an effect which is the opposite of soporific. However, with your guest's interests in mind, put a selection of books on the bedside table. It need hardly be added that they should be of a convenient size and weight for holding while lying down: paperbacks are well suited to this purpose.

Pictures should be fresh and bland; you can hardly go wrong with coloured prints of birds or flowers. A modern abstract painting which you admire yourself might have a perplexing, even an annoying effect on your guest. And just as he may like to glance sleepily at a book about the natural history of the district, so he might look at a local map. Ordnance Survey maps, supplied direct or through the bookshops, can be obtained to a scale as large as 25in to the mile. A framed map showing your cottage and the names of surrounding fields, woods, streams and public

The spare room

footpaths would be an adornment to the room; and might suggest to both you and your guest an expedition on foot which would ensure a good appetite for lunch, perhaps at an inn indicated by the mapmaker.

When you feel everything possible has been done, may I recommend that you sleep in your spare room for a night or so? A *Daily Telegraph* reader recently described having done this: 'I hadn't realised there was no switch on the bedside lamp and that one needed a long arm to reach down to the electric point to switch off; that the charming chintz curtains let in the lamplight from the road and early morning sun; that by pushing the narrow twin beds together it lessened the feeling that one might fall right and left; that by turning a table round one avoided vicious knocks'.

CHAPTER 11

The study

Study, like library, sounds almost too grand for a cottage, but all I have in mind is a bookish little room to which, if you don't live alone, you can decently retire.

The drawbacks to a study leading off the sitting room, which you might at first think ideal, are that you could appear unsociable to visitors and that you might be disturbed by voices audible through the intervening door. There is much to be said for the privacy of a study in an attic or even imposed on a spare bedroom—where the bed could be welcome. I can't help thinking, as I write, of the study of convention, sombre and full of trophies, where up to two generations ago the head of a household checked his wife's housekeeping accounts and grilled his daughters' suitors. Dons, schoolmasters and clergymen have them still. There's little chance of achieving such a room in a cottage, but, all the same, if you like the feeling of leather upholstery, dark velvet curtains and a coal fire in a Victorian grate, your study is the place for them: it is after all the room of one person only.

For writing, some people like the wide expanse of a

The study

rectangular table with space for piles of books and a typewriter; others prefer a bureau with pigeon holes and the means of shutting a flap on work in progress. A bureau has long capacious drawers, but the person sitting at it must lift the writing flap to get at the contents of the top drawer and move his legs back to pull out the lower drawers. The most satisfactory desk, in my own opinion, is the kneehole type which offers the elbow room of a table plus a wealth of drawers which are easy to reach.

The kneehole desk is universal in offices, and perhaps in many minds associated with them, but there are some which are domestic in feel. Much depends on the colour of the wood, the fashioning of drawer fronts, the style of handles and the treatment of the top. Some of the brass loop handles are very handsome, though small wooden ones had the blessing of late eighteenth-century architects. An insert of tooled green or amber leather as a writing surface can be a pleasure to hand and eye.

The obvious place for your table or desk is under the window, where you will have the maximum daylight and a view; but you will not necessarily like it there. Several study enthusiasts—Somerset Maugham for one—arranged for their windows to be set so high that visual distraction was impossible. Most of us like to be able to look through a window, if only to rest the eyes at intervals by focussing on something in the distance; my own preference is to have the outside world to one side of me, like the view available from a seat in a train. A disadvantage of a desk set directly before a window is that when the curtains are drawn the field of vision is blocked by what amounts to a blank wall; it can be pleasanter to have the desk a little farther back so that your eye, whenever you look up, takes in the objects in the room as well as the view outside. There is much to be said for a window which faces west

The study

and brings in sunlight when you may most welcome it—towards the end of the day.

A chair to go with the desk should be firm and of a height which allows the thighs to be parallel with the floor when you are sitting upright. A chair with arms is comfortable, but it tends to pin you behind your desk, being less easy to get up from than the armless kind. The sort of chair that swivels may help you to reach out to one side or behind, but seems to me to belong to the office.

Reading chair illustrated in A. J. Downing's *Architecture of Country Houses*, 1850

Where space permits, however grudgingly, a sofa could be regarded by a brain worker as a necessity for taking the short sleep which both Lloyd George and Winston Churchill found advisable at some time between the midday and evening meal. It might be good for thought, too. Plenty of people say their best thinking is done when horizontal (as, of course, in the bath).

The study

You may like to have in your study a convertible sofa-bed, a piece which dates from at least the first quarter of the nineteenth century, or its modern equivalent, the studio couch, and be able to adjust it on occasion for putting up a visitor for the night.

Box divan in octagonal room of nineteenth-century American cottage (Downing)

I will not attempt to make further suggestions for a room which should be very personal and reflect its owner's idiosyncrasies and his concern, or enviable lack of concern, for tidiness. He will know what he needs in the way of cupboards for files and periodicals, shelves for reference books and cabinets for specimens.

CHAPTER 12

Buying furniture

It is theoretically possible to buy everything needed for a cottage, from beds to the last place mat, in a single visit to a department store. The job might also be done at a fraction of the cost during one day at an auction sale. To judge for yourself, you have only to call at a saleroom and note the crowded variety of all household goods except the heavier bathroom equipment: though you may not want used pillows and blankets, you could get a sense of satisfaction from the purchase of a gas or electric cooker for £1 or of a scarcely trodden-on carpet for a third of the price elsewhere.

Some people, having moved into their cottage with the bare necessities, like to take their time in search of the furniture they really want, touring the local antique and junk shops, and attending auction sales. Plain, practical furniture can be selected from the catalogues of mail-order firms, who will deliver to your door.

In most country towns an auction sale is held every few weeks to dispose of about six hundred items. Dates and details of these, and of sales in private houses, are given in the local papers. You can, of course, ask firms of auctioneers to send you their catalogues. If you mean to buy a lot of things in a hurry you will probably need to spend most of the day in the saleroom, having previously viewed and marked in the catalogue the things you want. It need not be dull—some turn up at salerooms just for the spectacle and sense of restrained excitement—and you quickly learn about current values. You may hear someone remarking loudly as an article is announced that its support is riddled with woodworm, or asking the auctioneer, whose hammer is poised, if the top of something is really 'right' with the legs. You can guess that people who interrupt the bidding in this way are themselves potential buyers.

If you are interested in only a few of the lots, you will not find it necessary to spend much time in the saleroom, for it is possible to work out from the catalogue approximately when certain lots will be sold: most auctioneers get through from seventy to 100 an hour. If you cannot attend the sale yourself, you can ask one of the saleroom staff to bid for you, telling him the price to which you are prepared to go. He, or the auctioneer himself, will advise you about the bidding expected and the likelihood of antique dealers being interested.

Most of the stuff in ordinary salerooms is simply second-hand. But there will be antiques as well. An article is said to be an antique if it is over 100 years old; though the organisers of big antiques fairs accept only furniture made before 1830. A few well-chosen and serviceable antiques are a delight in a country cottage and gaining value all the time: this is something which does not happen with factory-made modern furniture.

Unfortunately antiques and near-antiques are disappearing steadily overseas, only the very finest pieces ever returning in the course of trade; and comparative scarcity means that even the humble Windsor chair, if demonstrably early in date, is by no means as reasonably priced as a few years ago. All the same, compare its price with a modern chair of the same type! Early country-made furniture of the sort which goes so well in cottages, including centuries-old oak pieces, can still be bought for surprisingly modest sums. It is not difficult to find an old round table with a pillar and three legs in oak or mahogany priced lower than its less pleasing modern equivalent. Vast quantities of these tables were made in the Georgian period and later.

When several fine pieces, worth hundreds of pounds, are being sold by auction, it sometimes happens that a group of dealers, to avoid pushing up the price, agree not to bid against one another and arrange for only one of their number to do the bidding. The question of which dealer takes the article home is decided afterwards at a private auction among themselves.

These rings, as they are called, operate especially at country house sales where sometimes neither vendor nor auctioneer is fully aware of the value of all the lots. In 1968 it was suggested that only a dealers' ring could explain the purchase in the country of a Duccio painting for £2,700 and its sale to the National Gallery six months later for £150,000. The operation of rings is less common at the big London salerooms where more experts and advisers are in attendance.

Rings have been illegal in Britain, though not in Northern Ireland, since the passing of the Auctions (Bidding Agreements) Act of 1927, reinforced by another of 1969 which increased the possible prison sentence from six months to two years. So far there has been no successful prosecution under either Act: the dealers make their agreements verbally and privately. However, the private

Buying furniture

buyer of household furniture need not worry about the rings, since in the main their effect is detrimental only to the owner of the goods and the auctioneer.

When they first go to auctions, some people are afraid of putting up a hand in case they get landed with something which will turn out to be an embarrassment. This can indeed happen. If a lot is knocked down to you, that is the end of it; you are the owner. But in the last resort you probably need not take it away. Having inspected it and been dismayed, you can ask the auctioneer, after paying him the amount bid, if he would mind including it in his next sale. He is almost certain to agree: you will have put him in the way of drawing two commissions on the same lot. In theory you could make a profit yourself in a few weeks' time, but for some reason it is a matter for celebration if this happens.

Antique shops are naturally a more expensive hunting-ground, because the dealer, who probably got his goods from a sale, needs to make a profit. But in these fascinating places you have a chance to pick and choose, to make up your mind at leisure, or to postpone making any decision for days while you find time to visit other shops. There is also the advantage that a dealer often gives useful advice, sharing his knowledge and experience. And he may let you take a piece home on approval so that you can be sure it suits your room; but, if he does not know you well, it is reasonable to hand him a returnable sum of money.

There are two main types of antique dealer, the professional, who could be a member of the British Antique Dealers' Association, and the semi-amateur. Of course, the latter is professional in the sense that he is paid, but he cannot rely on his dealing for a living and may not know much about the articles he deals in.

The rich semi-amateur is often a collector at heart and

Buying furniture

may be noticeably unwilling to part with certain articles in his shop. This kind of antique dealer is to be found in numerous provincial towns all over Britain. His shop, with a gothic-lettered sign, is sometimes the front room of a substantial old house or an out-house in its grounds. There may not be many goods on show, but they will be pleasantly arranged and will have been dusted and polished. You may find there, as a focal point, either floodlit shelves or a Georgian dumbwaiter containing a selection of good though highly priced glass and porcelain. Occasionally the prices are marked in a code which even the assistant, if there is one, must seek help to decipher; but this putting-off device does not necessarily mean that potential customers are told the price which their appearance indicates they might pay.

The semi-amateur dealer who is not rich (and probably has another occupation) acts as a scavenger at sales; he goes on accumulating his bargains, planning to do them up, but very often he loses heart and lets them lie about in a jumbled mass with the lot numbers still on them. It's worth having a look round, if you are in need of a cheap table of a particular size, or a spare electric fire.

Another stamping ground of this type of semi-amateur is one of the antique supermarkets which emerged in the early 1960s. The idea for these came from the indoor markets of the Portobello Road in London, spreading to Camden Town, Chelsea and elsewhere. The owner of an ex-warehouse or store partitions off as many stall areas as possible and lets them for a day, week, month or year to dealers, many of whom specialise in a particular line: snuff boxes, barometers, firearms or gramophones. Oddities rather than antiques are what you generally find at these stalls; but you may come across something you would be glad to have.

Buying furniture

The professional dealers have to make a steady profit and from time to time quite a big one: antiques are their living. Some of the articles they deal in never actually appear in their shops, but are kept aside for collectors and other dealers whom they believe will be ready to give a good price. They have a knowledge of antiques acquired by study and experience of the trade. They may give customers interesting information, explaining what they know about the origin of a piece; and they won't deliberately hide flaws, for they have a reputation to keep. Their stock is sometimes dirty and ill-arranged, but bargain-hunters discover that nothing is going for a song.

At the bottom end of the secondhand trade is the true junk shop, noticeable as you drive through a country town because of the curious collection of items set outside on the pavement. These have been known to include a respectable chair or two, an abandoned bath, or a sundial. A builder's yard can also produce some useful surprises.

Old and secondhand furniture, wherever bought, will often show signs of woodworm damage caused by the larvae of the furniture beetle. The holes may not be active, but all of them should be liberally brushed over with an insecticide liquid; it need not be laboriously injected into every hole, for the fumes have a deadly penetration. It is a good idea to repeat this treatment in May before the annual emergence of larvae in June and July. If left unchecked, the beetles are liable to spread, laying eggs in the crevices of furniture, floors, banisters and even in books. In time the boring will take all the strength from a piece of wood—many a chair leg has collapsed beneath a sitter. Walnut and beech are especially liable to attack by the furniture beetle, mahogany and oak less so.

Its presence is shown unmistakably by a fine wood dust which drifts to the floor and appears when the piece of furniture is tapped. In *Restoring Junk*, 1970, Suzanne Beedell says that a furniture dealer she knows 'made an absolute fortune by always carrying a bag of wood powder in his pocket, and surreptitiously depositing a small heap of it beneath each object he wished to buy, and then drawing the attention of other dealers, particularly strangers, to this irrefutable evidence'.

There are usually other little jobs to carry out when you bring home old furniture—giving it a good scrub, perhaps, or renewing a chair cover. In general, it is best not to attempt major repairs, but a piece of furniture which is slightly broken or no longer rigid can probably be put right by glueing—after cleaning the parts first—or by replacing old nails, screws or dowel pins.

If the drawers of a chest of drawers refuse to move easily, it will work wonders to run candle grease or soap along the sliding edges. But, unless you are personally skilled as a furniture restorer, it is best for an expert to supply missing table legs and chair arms and deal with warped panels, buckled veneers and incomplete marquetry and mouldings.

Restoring the surface of sound pieces can often be quite easy. Don't be in a hurry to strip off and start again; washing and then polishing an existing patina may prove much more satisfactory. However, French polish, detectable by the fact that it softens under methylated spirits, may have crazed to an extent which makes it not worth keeping. You could take it off yourself with ammonia or a varnish solvent and either put on new French polish or rub repeatedly with wax.

For bad heat marks on French polish, it is worth trying linseed oil and then turpentine. Superficial marks and the white patches and rings caused by spilt spirits can generally be removed completely—and more safely than with a

Page 103 Interior of an unimproved cottage—with cottager—photographed in the 1930s. In foreground, the upper part of a balloon-back chair

Page 104 Kitchens: *(above)* pots—one with tap—suspended over open wood fire; foot-level oven; *(below)* modern units in a converted cottage lose character to convenience

Buying furniture

solvent—by careful rubbing with an abrasive paste. But tips galore can be found in several recently-published books on the mending and maintaining of old furniture.

To gather together the basic essentials needed in your cottage, it may be necessary to visit the nearest town, or you may find nearly everything in the village general stores. It is easy to forget things and have to make unnecessary journeys. The list below, omitting consumables like bulbs, soap and matches, is offered as a guide for a three-bedroom cottage to be inhabited by two people. It starts with a tool of great versatility, the large screwdriver, not the least of its uses being that of levering out tintacks left in floors by previous occupants.

1 large screwdriver, small screwdriver for electrical fittings, hammer, box of assorted screws and nails, tool for making screw holes, box of rawlplugs, pliers
Lamp shades
1 soft indoor broom, dustpan and brush, yard broom
1 carpet sweeper, 2 dusters
3 washing up cloths, 3 tea towels, 1 floor cloth
6 personal towels, 2 bath mats, 1 stout nail brush
1 large dust bin, pedal bin for kitchen waste
1 bathroom mirror, lavatory brush
3 wastepaper baskets
1 laundry basket
1 coal scuttle, shovel, poker
1 plate rack
1 tin opener, corkscrew, 3 ashtrays
1 kettle, frying pan, 3 saucepans of assorted sizes
1 teapot, tea tray
Lidded containers for tea, sugar and butter
2 sharp knives for peeling and carving, 1 wooden spoon
Bowls and jugs for preparing and serving food
6 each of large table knives, small knives, table forks,

Buying furniture

     dessert forks, table spoons, dessert spoons, teaspoons
- 6 each of dinner plates, dessert plates, side plates, cups, saucers, egg cups
- 6 tumblers, claret glasses, 2 tooth glasses, 1 water jug
- 10 sheets, 12 blankets, 3 bedspreads
- 6 pillows, 10 pillow slips

CHAPTER 13

The garden

The garden of a non-village cottage commonly consists of about an eighth of an acre, bumpy with forsaken diggings. As its new owner, you may want to make radical changes. In the small compass at your disposal, what you do to your garden reflects yourself as surely as how you furnish the cottage.

A garden that straggles to a point beside a lane is a reminder of how the old cottagers acquired more land: by infiltration and illicit enclosure of road verge. Extra square feet were valuable to a poor labourer, who needed for his family all the vegetables he could get and a place for fowls and a pig. Such flowers as lupins and poppies were incidentals which had to take care of themselves.

If yours is a former labourer's garden, you could make it a thing of beauty with herbaceous borders, climbers and flowering shrubs; but unless you employ a gardener the work would eat up time you might rather devote to something else. I want to suggest that your garden could be made to give great pleasure in return for a nominal amount of work.

The garden

The sort of garden I have in mind is secluded and mostly green—a place for relaxation and occasional meals; its only border is a row of herbs by the kitchen door; it is both an outdoor room and an extension of the countryside. There may be roses round the cottage door and clematis or honeysuckle round the windows, but the garden has few boastful blooms to prevent it blending with neighbouring fields and woods. It has no rockery (not, anyway, in a rockless part of the country) and no waterfalls kept going with a pump; it is just a plot surrounded by a stout thorn hedge and containing hardly anything but grass, a few old apple trees and perhaps a quince.

A virtue of mature trees is that they need no pruning, though initial repairs and propping may be necessary. The hedge and the grass call for cutting, certainly, but there is something very satisfactory about leaving part of the grass uncut, creating a contrast between mown lawn and an area allowed to grow long and shelter wild flowers. Orchard grass which has had its winter trim makes an ideal base for a heartening spring display of snowdrops, crocuses, scillas and any of the varieties of daffodil. The bulbs can be bought by the sack and, once put in, bloom year after year without anything being done.

The smaller village garden, perhaps behind a terrace cottage, may be just a lumpily cultivated back yard when you take it over. Yet it could soon be green and restful, for there will surely be room for one tree and a bit of lawn. But first of all see to the enclosure of your plot, bearing in mind that everyone feels free to address comments and questions to a householder, however occupied, who is on view in his garden. Building a wall from scratch is expensive unless done by yourself, though much nicer than a fence. The high wall—say 6ft—surrounding a cottage plot scarcely bigger than a room is a characteristically English

The garden

amenity—and what a calming sense of ownership and seclusion it provides, especially on a summer's evening when you sit outside.

You need not assume that next-door neighbours will raise objections to the building or raising of a party wall. I suggest from experience that they are more likely to be pleased; after all, you will be making them a present of extra privacy for themselves and another place on which to train their roses.

Whatever the size of your garden, when you start to think about its furniture it is a good idea to find a place for a garden bench which is not immediately visible from the cottage. A semi-screen of bushes, with possibly a hurdle at the back while they grow, will not only create a sheltered nook for sitting in, but add an element of mystery to the smallest garden by making it impossible to see the whole of it at once. Garden seats which can stay out all the time are readily procured new and secondhand. If they are to be painted, as iron ones must be, dark green generally looks better than white in a country setting. Plain, never-peeling wood can be the most satisfactory of all: teak is especially good as it resists rot and keeps its shape through many summers and winters. A solid table of teak and chairs to match encourage the taking of meals out of doors. If you have room to store them, wicker chairs are comfortable, and light to carry. Cane seats, bamboo tables and perhaps an old basket-weave chaise-longue sometimes turn up in the saleroom and can be painted for use in the garden. More permanent seats can be formed with slabs of stone. Is there a place for a wide-seated children's swing? Suspended from the best bough of an apple tree, swings are far from unsightly and, if chain rather than rope is employed, they should never need attention.

As for folding garden furniture, the shops have never

The garden

been better stocked than in the last few years. Although the deck chair remains the popular standby, and is also the one that folds up flattest, it no longer remains the most comfortable of the collapsible chairs. There are daybeds in metal alloys and PVC, adjustable at head and foot, which are most ingenious inventions. For comfort on a hot day, however, particularly when sunbathing, canvas covers are infinitely preferable to PVC; canvas is kinder to the body and does not scorch you after being left out in the sun.

Unless there is space in your all-purpose downstairs cloakroom, where to store your portable chairs and garden tools can be a difficulty, particularly if a wooden shed looks unsightly in a very small garden and there is no garage. A solidly-built old privy could be adapted into a useful storage shed, though you may be obliged to strip it of an endearing double seat with one part for a child, the other for a grown-up. The merit of most of these tile-roofed miniature buildings is that they were made of the same materials as the cottage; they clearly belong and take well to being masked a little with creepers. Some cottage gardens still contain a small brick pig pound, which can be used as a shed.

Statuary of any kind rarely looks right in a cottage garden, nor do classical urns on plinths. On the other hand a bird bath or an old stone sundial could be a modest-looking object of interest at the bottom of the garden. For those with a mind to learn more about sundials and their long history there is Sir Alan Herbert's book, *Sundials Old and New*, published in 1967.

I have advocated minimal gardening work. There are some walled-in back yards which can be made into gardens requiring no work at all. Or no more than a window box. All you do is pave the whole area with old bricks or squares of stone, fill in the cracks with cement and sand to prevent

The garden

plant growth, train Virginia creeper up the walls—this is one of the few creepers which cling unaided—and distribute a few tubs of geraniums or petunias. Coopers' barrels, complete or cut in half, are on sale in most country districts and make attractive containers. Appropriately holed, they can be used for strawberry plants.

In such a garden you can sit at ease and drink your wine, aware that no horticultural task awaits your attention. There is no possibility here of sweating over beds and borders 'to avoid our neighbours' reproach'. The phrase is from Adrian Bell, who wrote in *Suffolk Harvest* of the happiest days he had spent the previous summer.

> They were the days in which I sat in my meadow... a wild flower garden. For this all you need is a natural sward round your house. When I pass a house newly erected in a meadow, and see the zealous owner in his shirtsleeves, with stakes and measuring line and spade, starting to make a garden, I want to plead with him, 'Don't do it. You are destroying that heaven-sent gift, Nature's garden, which is at your door. In return you are dooming yourself to hours of recurrent backaching toil with fork and hoe.'

Once the meadow has been carved up Nature will not return and take possession in the same gracious fashion. A forsaken garden is not Nature; it is Nature run amok. To revert to a native sward and a native hedgerow, to daisied lawns and dog roses, needs a husbandly effort. Then when you have obtained your field again, with orchard trees in it, you can look a dandelion in the eye and feel jolly, which you never could before you banished the word weed from your vocabulary.

CHAPTER 14

The coming of cottage furniture

Until around 1850 the furniture of most rural cottages consisted of crude stools and chests supplemented by built-in cupboards. A few rush-bottomed chairs would have been prized possessions, as would a cumbersome table or press discarded from a farmhouse. The fact that life in a cottage was rough and overcrowded may be suggested still by massive wear on the floor near the fireplace, fragments of innumerable plates and mugs in the soil by the back entrance, a sagging upper floor scored all over by the supports of bedding, which slept a dozen or more together.

Rural labourers could not afford to buy furniture. In any case it was rarely made specifically for small rooms unless by the hands of a cottager himself. The nice country pieces known as cottage antiques are unlikely to have begun their existence in a cottage unless its occupant was a well-to-do tradesman, a parson, a lady in reduced circumstances, or a literary figure like Goldsmith, Wordsworth or Coleridge. The cottage antiques of today were in the farm houses, the lesser houses in provincial towns and the village street houses of men of property.

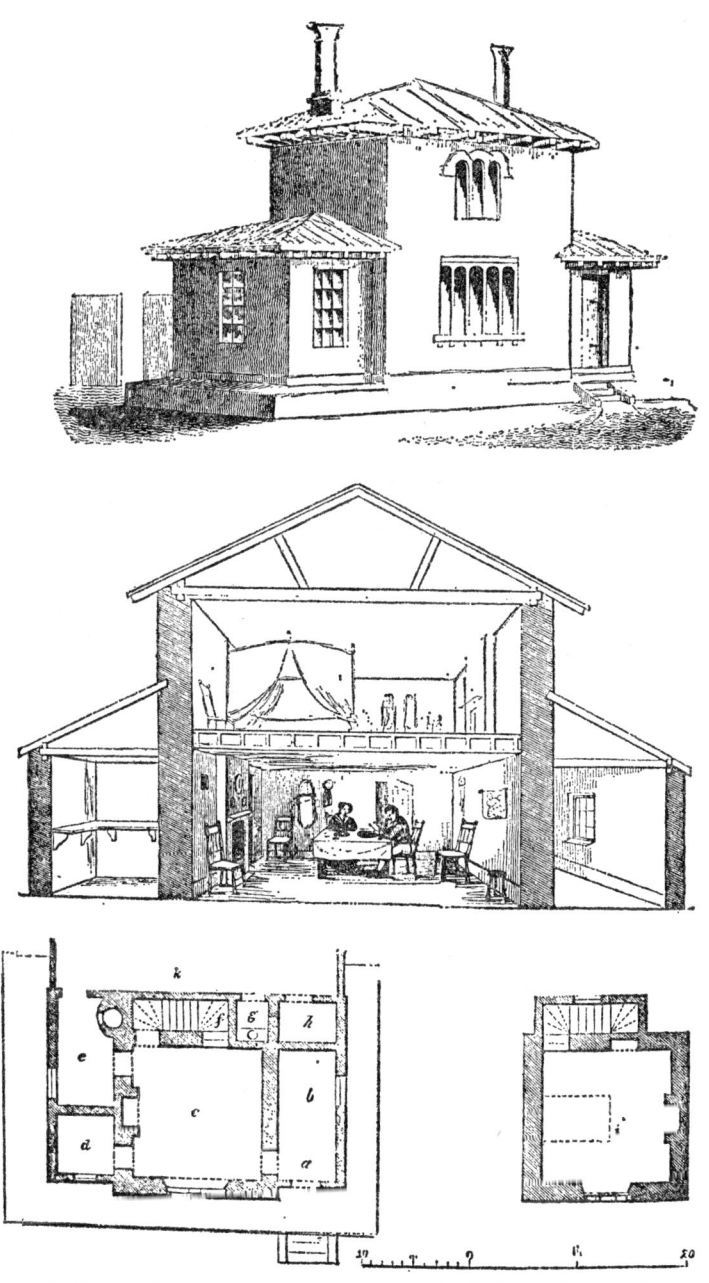

Italian-style cottage shown in Loudon's *Encyclopaedia*

The coming of cottage furniture

Cottage furniture—specialised articles bought in the towns or made up to order—gradually emerged in the nineteenth century. J. C. Loudon's *Encyclopaedia of Cottage, Farm and Villa Architecture*, published in 1833, helped greatly to popularise contemporary inventions for cottages, but decades passed before there were railways to help distribute the new purpose-built cottage furnishings.

Loudon gathered ideas assiduously. Eighty-two of the *Encyclopaedia*'s densely-packed pages are devoted to advice on the furnishing of cottages, with over 200 illustrations on which Loudon comments, often comparing one design unfavourably with another. What he offered, in fact, was a popular catalogue of household objects. Only it was hardly popular in the strict sense.

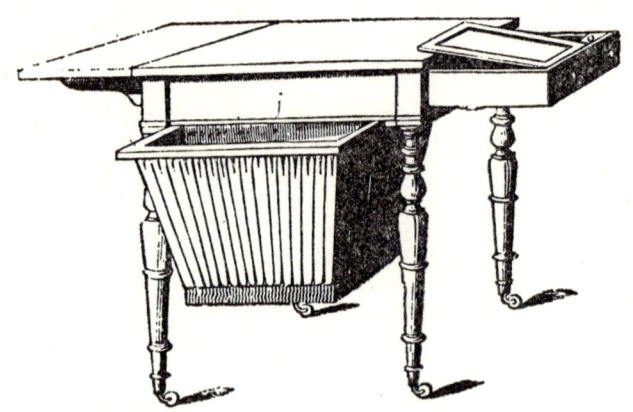

Multi-purpose table for cottagers (Loudon)

Ordinary poor cottagers, could they have seen the book, would have found much of the furniture so far from their ambitions as to be meaningless. But Loudon was not addressing them; he was addressing employers and landlords whom he earnestly wished to make more considerate. He had no illusions. 'The Furniture and Furnishing of

The coming of cottage furniture

Cottages have been hitherto neglected in every country where the comfort of the cottager has depended on those above him.' He anticipated criticism. 'If it should be asked, whether we expect that such Designs as those which follow can be executed or procured by the cottagers of this country, we answer that we trust they soon will be; and we believe that the first step towards this desirable end is to teach them what to wish for.'

The book was well subscribed among the gentry and undoubtedly some landlords were at once inspired to order from their estate joiners new furniture for the use of those who depended on them. But in the long run it was the furniture makers who took most notice of Loudon's observations on furniture—his *Encyclopaedia* ran through edition after edition, becoming for about fifty years a treasured book of reference for tradesmen.

If some of the furniture illustrated seems today very ugly—in particular the Gothic bedsteads and cradles and the massive Elizabethan-style chairs—it has to be remembered that Loudon was compiling his great work at a time when the Georgian classic tradition was fading away in favour of designs with a romantic, old English appeal. Loudon approved the trend. He admired the pointed angles of the Gothic style in architecture. In encouraging the introduction of these into furniture—often in the form of mere trivial ornament—he guilelessly helped to make Gothic a commercially successful fashion and hastened the descent of furniture design in general into ill-proportioned showiness.

Aesthetic considerations apart, it must be said that Loudon's recommendations for cottages are based on commonsense and human convenience. This is shown, I think, by the illustrations included in this book.

One reason for an immediate impact enjoyed by the

American cottage furniture for bedrooms, shown in Downing's *Architecture of Country Houses*

The coming of cottage furniture

Encyclopaedia is that it came out at a time when the gentry were dallying with a literary interest in cottages as picturesque ingredients in a landscape, and also as ventures in tenants' housing which could be a credit to a rich man's estate and the envy of his neighbours.

Picturesque cottages were being built at this time as retreats in which the rich man himself could play at leading an innocent, rustic life. However, his carefully sited country cottage would be big enough for four servants and include, half-concealed at the back, a double coach house. Several of Jane Austen's characters repaired to cottages of this type. The very word cottage was already fashionable—significantly it is given precedence to 'farm' and 'villa' in the title of Loudon's book—and its aura was not to escape the emergent furniture manufacturers when writing their advertisements.

Loudon's example as a reformer of domestic interiors was followed in America by A. J. Downing. His *Architecture of Country Houses*, 1850, incorporates with adequate acknowledgement many of Loudon's engravings and follows on a smaller scale the general plan of the *Encyclopaedia*. Downing, however, addressed his cottagers directly. 'In this country,' he wrote (meaning mainly the eastern states), 'the majority of cottages are occupied not by tenants, dependants or serfs, as in many parts of Europe, but by industrious and intelligent mechanics and working men, the bone and sinew of the land, who own the ground on which they stand, build them for their own use and arrange them to satisfy their own tastes.'

Downing took his role as a style-setter very seriously and offered his fellow Americans detailed advice on achieving in their cottages 'a tasteful simplicity of decoration to harmonise with the character of the building'. This character was commonly provided by either the Gothic or the

The coming of cottage furniture

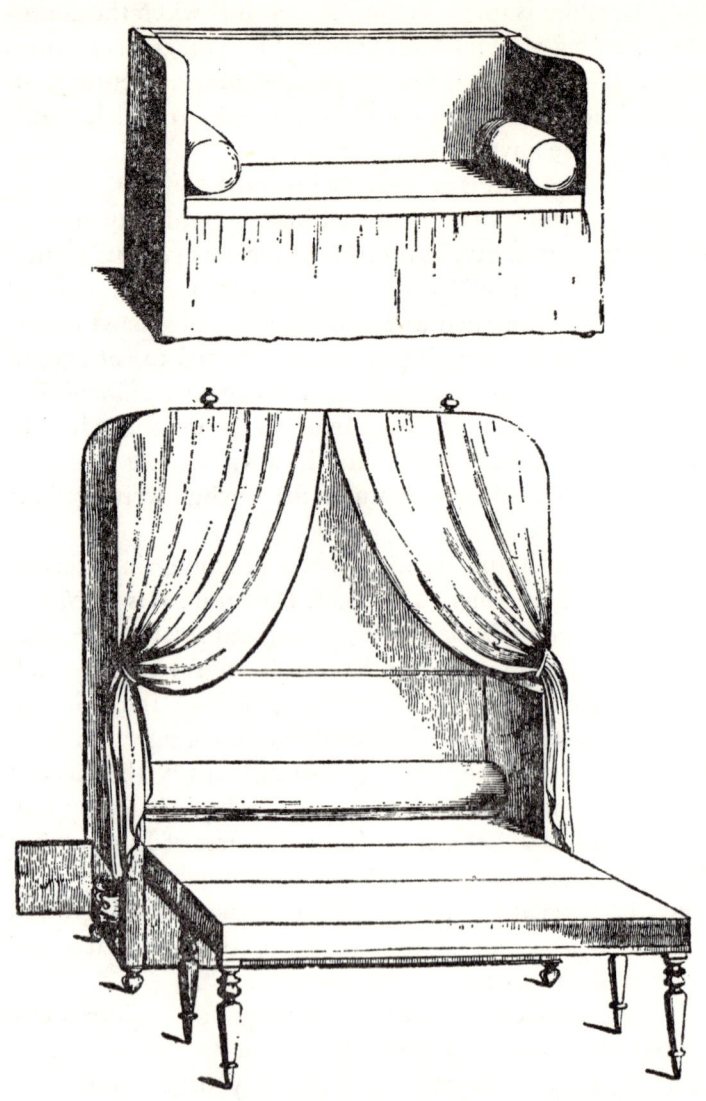

Sofa-bed to save space: *(above)* the piece as a sofa; *(below)* unfolded and assembled to form a bed (Loudon)

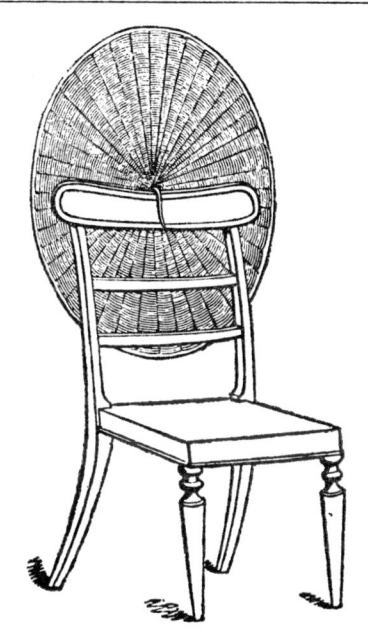

Straw firescreen fitted to dining-room chair (Loudon)

Italian style in building. Downing recommended as a first step in cottage embellishment the tacking-on of a veranda: this gave status, he said, in indicating to all 'a constant means of enjoyment for the inmates of the cottage—something in their daily lives besides ministering to the necessities'.

He suggested, as Loudon did, white interior walls and ceilings, or, for a better effect, fawn or grey walls with white ceilings. He wrote, too, of 'the cheerful, cottage-like expression' produced by the hanging of paper in living rooms. 'In some countries—England, for example—papered walls are objectionable on account of their retaining dampness in a moist climate. But in the United States there is no complaint of this kind.'

The coming of cottage furniture

As for cottage furniture, said Downing, it could scarcely be too simple, chaste or unpretending in its character; it should not resemble town furniture. He congratulated American cabinet makers on having begun to turn out furniture suitable for cottages, and on arranging for it to be available in all the principal cities. 'One can now furnish a cottage at short notice without having it look as if it had been stuffed with chairs and tables sent up from a town house five times its size.'

But Downing also offered instructions for making cottage furniture at home. 'The simplest and cheapest kind of furniture by which an air of taste may be given to a cottage consists of a plain box or bench, made of boards by the hands of the master of the dwelling, stuffed with hay, corn husks, moss or hair, held in place by a covering of coarse canvas, or covered in chintz by the mistress of the cottage.' The next stage was to add square cushions to give the sitter support for his back without it touching the wall. The finished article can be seen in the illustration of an octagonal cottage room.

A rather strident staining or brown-painting of anything made of wood was a characteristic, like the abundant draperies, of the average, newly appointed, mid-nineteenth-century cottage on both sides of the Atlantic. Furniture of 'ordinary' beech or deal would be made mahogany red, rosewood pink or walnut yellow-orange by staining. Treatment with brown paint was generally reserved for doors, window frames, the wainscot, skirting boards, even floor surrounds. These parts were grained—that is, painted with a degree of skill to imitate the grain of another wood. Sometimes cement and plaster were so treated. Loudon approved of graining; he considered it in good taste to imitate with the paint brush the beauty of oak and chestnut. 'All woodwork avowed as such,' he wrote, 'should if

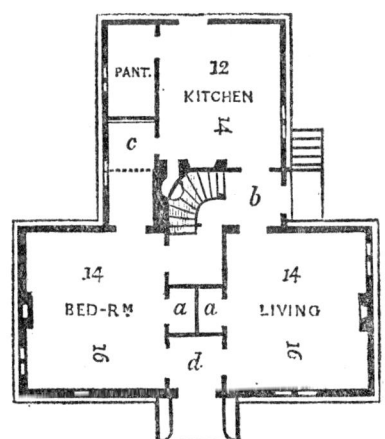

New England cottage (Downing)

possible be grained in imitation of some natural wood; not with a view to having the imitation mistaken for the original, but rather to create allusion to it, and by a diversity of lines and shades, to produce a kind of variety and intricacy which affords pleasure to the eye.'

Downing was equally in favour of making cottage woodwork resemble a local hardwood. 'The grained surface, being made smooth by varnishing, does not readily become soiled, and when it does, a moment's application of a damp cloth will make all clean and bright.'

Loudon had a lot to say about carpets. He considered fully-fitted carpet a great source of comfort in a cottage and the most satisfactory of all floor coverings, but he allowed that this was uneconomical because it could not be turned. 'A square carpet may be changed eight times, so as to be worn equally on every part of both sides; a circular one indefinitely.' In choosing a pattern, the smallest was generally to be preferred because, as well as suiting small rooms, a carpet with a small pattern needed less cutting in sewing the lengths together so that they matched. 'The parlour carpet, and the carpet of at least one bedroom, should be of the same pattern, in order that the latter may be used to mend it; because it is always bad, both in point of effect and economy, to mend what is old with what is quite new.' He went on to explain at some length that if a carpet of brilliant hue was put down, some part of the walls or the curtains must be ornamented with the same colour to achieve harmony.

Loudon had seen an article about 'geographical carpets' in the *Mechanics Magazine* and quoted it with approval '... a carpet is so admirably adapted to geographical instruction, that it may be almost said to be a natural article for the purpose... A family in the daily occupation of a room furnished with such a carpet would acquire unavoidably a more permanent knowledge of a given portion of the earth than could be obtained by any other means.' There is no evidence that carpets marked with the lines of a map ever became common; but maps pasted to walls, and wallpapers printed with useful information, have at all times been valued.

There exist paintings and engravings which give a good idea of what cottages often looked like indoors in the nineteenth century. If you could see a picture of the interior of your own cottage after dark, you might well wonder why it had not long ago burned down. The branches blazing on the hearth and the uncertain flames of rushlights or crude candles would seem in all-too-close proximity to shelf valances and frilly curtains moving to and fro in the draught.

CHAPTER 15

Furnishing to let

Unlike weekend visitors, furnished tenants have a right to make demands and complaints, and they are liable, when you are not there, to have accidents. An insurance policy which covers third party risks is only a longstop. So, when you make preparations to let your cottage, try to ensure that it is without structural and other faults capable of causing injury.

Obviously you would not knowingly let the cottage with dangerous defects—fragile sections of an upper floor, a flue able to leak fumes, faulty wiring—but you might possibly, well knowing yourself how to escape mishaps, expect too much of your tenant. Explain peculiarities by all means (though don't expect the information to reach your tenants' visitors) and, where it seems essential, clear yourself of responsibility by pinning up a few notices; but your main effort should go into making everything reasonably foolproof.

Be especially careful to avoid arrangements which could help to cause a fire or feed the flames once a fire had broken out. Here are some potentially dangerous things: an oil

Furnishing to let

heater left in a draughty place where it might flare up; petrol, paraffin, old newspapers and rags stored together in the under-stairs cupboard; irons and other appliances equipped for plugging into light sockets instead of wall points; trailing or badly frayed flexes; an electric toaster sited near curtains or inflammable materials; loose switches on gas or electric cookers; damaged power points; open fires not provided with guards.

Ideally, the only notice you might want to pin up would be a list of useful telephone numbers: tradesmen, doctor, taxi driver, garage, local livestock owner, plumber—with perhaps a line at the end giving the whereabouts of the main stopcock.

No sleight of hand should be expected of tenants in connection with operating the water supply; they should not have to draw water with a bucket from a deep well or, worse still, keep children away from a disused well concealed by long grass in the garden. No special instructions should be necessary about what to do in the event of the roof leaking or the fireplace smoking, no tricks should have to be imparted about the operation of your electricity, gas, drains or cooking appliances.

At one period, I received from a cottage tenant a number of long typewritten letters about my electric fires and flexes. I also recall correspondence with a man—who came with his wife for a summer fortnight—about the small size of my dustbin. Were there, I was asked, any cardboard boxes to help out, could they buy for the cottage a second dustbin, which type would I prefer, might its price be deducted from the rent? I could easily have spared myself these letters—from people who were good, careful tenants. I now see that the bad tenant, maltreating your property, affronting neighbours and ceasing to send rent, is unlikely, for fear of prompting a visit, to write any letters at all.

Furnishing to let

As few estate agents are prepared to undertake the bother of handling furnished cottages in the country, the usual way of finding a tenant, for a long or a short let, is to advertise in a newspaper and select as well as you can from the ones who respond. You may favour someone elderly on the grounds that he won't knock the furniture about or spill drinks on the carpets, or you may prefer someone young, who you think will be good at coping with an emergency like a burst tank or cattle breaking into the garden.

As there is always an outside chance of disappointment in letting to strangers, there are certain preliminary steps worth taking. A reference obtained from an applicant's bank, his firm and an individual of social standing (ringing the people up if necessary) could alter or pleasantly confirm your choice. The signing of a tenancy agreement offers a measure of protection: your solicitor would be glad to tailor-make an impressive document incorporating all your wishes, but there is a standard form, to be had from any branch of the Solicitors' Law Stationery Society, which covers all the usual points like replacing broken articles and not altering the structure of the cottage. It is essential to prepare in duplicate an inventory of the contents and agree it with the tenant before handing him the keys.

However much confidence you may have in your chosen tenant, you will want to minimise the opportunities for wear and tear. Put washable loose covers on chairs and sofas, where necessary; see that valuable and breakable articles, and watercolour pictures affected by sunlight, are either removed or locked in a cupboard. Precautions of this sort will help the tenant's peace of mind as well as yours.

One of the blessings of letting a country cottage, is that most tenants are only too glad to put in some physical exercise in the garden and prevent it from becoming a tangle; so the better the grass-cutting and other implements you leave behind the better everything is likely to look when you next see your garden. An easy means of watering might encourage the tenant to save the life of newly planted fruit trees, and a sound and accessible ladder help him to clear gutters blocked with leaves and birds' debris. Don't worry too much if an enthusiastic young couple digs a pattern of flower beds on the lawn, for these can be easily turfed over later; but do remember to say a few words about existing plants which you would be sorry to have dug up or mutilated.

Where the main purpose of owning a cottage is to derive an income from letting it for family holidays, making good deficiencies and providing sound, efficient equipment are clearly more important than the visual appeal of the fabrics. Linen is not provided in the case of a long let, but for periods of less than a month sheets, pillowcases and towels should be left for the tenants. Short-term tenants won't mind about an ill-proportioned bedside table or an ugly headboard, but they will not be happy if a mattress has hollows in it and there are too few blankets.

Serviceable furnishings are what you need for letting purposes, quantity coming before high quality. It doesn't matter, for example, how ordinary the crockery is so long as there is enough of it and it is in good repair. Remove or mend all insecure furniture: an imperfectly cane-seated chair which must be sat on in a certain way generally survives two days of a tenancy.

Auction salerooms are the best places to gather the furnishings for a holiday cottage which must show a profit. If you go along prepared to bid for any robust table, chest of drawers or easy chair of the right size—without worrying about aesthetic considerations—you may be amazed to

Furnishing to let

find how inexpensive some secondhand furniture can be, the prices received hardly covering, you may suspect, the vendor's cost in transporting it to the saleroom. An auctioneer will have to work hard, sometimes, to raise £3 for a set of dining chairs made in the 1930s or 40s. I saw this happen at a sale only the other day when six rather dreary-looking oak chairs with rexine-covered, drop-in seats came up for sale; yet as proper strong chairs you could tilt back on after a meal they would have been a useful buy—and easy to re-cover.

I have already referred to the extraordinarily low sums paid at auction for a perfectly satisfactory cooker. Trifling bids are made for refrigerators, domestic water heaters, garden furniture and tools. Curtains, too, seldom attract much bidding. If you want new, fresh-looking curtains, without having to make them, they can be bought ready-made, lined or unlined, at department stores and from direct-mail firms, in a wide choice of size, colour and material.

The cottage-to-let-furnished should not be handed over to a tenant until you have tried it out in every respect yourself. Remember you are being paid for a service and that all tenants are customers; moreover, you can reflect for your just gratification that their mere presence means you have succeeded, in one way or another, in furnishing your country cottage.

Acknowledgements

I would like to thank the interior decorator Mrs Campbell Gibson and my aunt Peggy Hickman for manuscript-reading and helpful suggestions, and my wife for curbing fanciful theories. I also want to thank Mr George Weaver and Mr Ian Gambrill for professional photographing of more cottage rooms than it has been possible to use. Mr Alan Taylor's book *Making the Most of Colour in the Home* has been referred to with profit.

Index

Adam, Robert, 75
Advertising a cottage to let, 126
Andirons, 38, 78
Antique shops, 67, 99-101
Antiques, 17, 21, 56-7, 68, 89, 97
Antique supermarkets, 100
Architecture of Country Houses (1850), 117, 119-122
Architraves, 61
Auction sales, 41, 53, 55, 59, 63, 67, 96-9, 127-8
Auctions (Bidding Agreements) Act, 98
Ants and other intruding insects, 22, 23
Austen, Jane, 117

Balloon-back chairs, 17, 73
Basket grates, 38, 78
Bathrooms (1970), 80
Bathroom walls, 36
Baths and basins, 79-82
Beardmores, 57
Bedroom chairs, 73, 88
Beds, 26, 55; metric sizes for, 55; bunk, 59; guest room, 87; in a study, 92; in a cottage to let, 127
Bedside tables, 56, 88, 127

Bedspread, 56
Beech, 48, 101
Beedell, Suzanne, 102
Bell, Adrian, 111
Benches and stools, 73, 75
Bidets, 81
Birds, damage by, 22
Blankets and suitcases, storage for, 54
Bookcases and bookshelves, 32, 37, 40-1, 51, 62, 90
Books, secondhand, bought in bulk, 41; guest room, 90
Bowls of flowers, 65, 89
Box beds, 17
Box toilet glasses, 58, 59
Bread ovens, unblocking, 15; procedure for operating, 42, 43; within hearth, 52
Brick and stone floors, 27, 43
British Antique Dealers' Association, 99
Bucknell, Barry, 84
Builders and workmen, 15, 82
Builders' yards, useful articles to be found in, 101
Bureaux, 68, 93
Burglars, 21

131

Index

Candles, 16, 71, 77, 89, 90, 123
Candlesticks, 17, 89
Card table, 68
Carpets, close-fitting and squares of, 28-30; bedroom, 55; bathroom, 83; early 19th-century views on, 122, 123
Carriage lamps, 17-18
Cast iron grates, 40
Cedar, 58
Ceilings, 17, 37, 38, 46; problems of sloping, 53, 56; low 38, 71
Ceramic tiles, 29
Chesterfields, 69, 85
Chests, storage of blankets in, 58; mule, 59
Chests of drawers, built in, 54; two-section, 56; antique, 57; servants', 57-8; military, 58; spare bedroom, 88; lubricating runners of, 102
Chiffoniers, 75
Childrens' bedroom, 59
Chimney corners, 15, 17, 77
China, displaying of, 77
Cloakrooms, 84
Clutter, 16
Coathangers, 54
Cobbett, William, 68
Collecting works of art, 18, 21
Colour and pattern, 64
Colour wheel, The, 64
Complementary colours, 65
Concrete floors, 27
Condensation, 36, 80
Continental hip bath, 79
Cookers, 45, 46, 96, 125
Cooking pots of the past, 77
Copper jugs, 17
Cork tiles, 83
Corner cupboards, 77
Corners, uneasy effect of furniture placed across, 68
Corner shelves, 52
Country Chippendale chairs, 68

Country furniture, 17, 43, 47-9, 68
Cottages, labourers', 15; 'cultured', 16; a gamekeeper's, 19; semi-detached, 25; terrace, 25; main-road, 25; timber-framed, 26; Regency, 33; Picturesque, 117
Cream paint, 32
Cupboards, 40, 46; built-in hanging, 53-4; built in drinks, 63
Curtain rails and rods, 32
Curtains, 16, 32, 35, 65, 82-3, 87-8, 91-3; ready-made, 128
Cushions, 58; to introduce colour, 65; to protect walls, 120

Daily Telegraph, The, 91
Dampness, remedies for, 23, 37
Daylight, disadvantages of facing when in bed, 56
Deal (pine), 57, 120
Dealers' rings, 98
Dealers in old furniture, types of 98-100
Demolition contractors, as a source of seasoned wood, 63
Department stores, 96
Desks, 68
Dining chairs, 73, 128
Dining tables, 71-3
Dog, sleeping place for, 84
Door furniture, 32, 52
Door mat, 26
Doors, framed and panelled, 32; ledged and braced, 62; second-hand, 63
Double-glazing, 24
Downing, A. J., 94-5, 117, 119-22
Draughts, 17, 24, 27
Dressers, 48, 76
Dressing tables, 56
Dry rot, 37, 63

132

Index

Dumbwaiters, 76, 100
Easy chairs, 69
Eiderdown, 58
Electric blankets, 90
Electric fires, 54, 77; in bathroom, 81, in spare bedroom, 89
Electric light, from wall and ceiling lamps, 46, 59, 64, 82, 84
Electricity, power points for, 15, 91; lack of, 19; in the bathroom, 81-2; faulty wiring for, 124
Electric torch, 90
Elm, 48, 76
Emulsion paint, 31
Encyclopaedia of Cottage, Farm and Villa Architecture (1833), 114-15, 117, 122-3
Extractor fan for bathroom, 80

Faggot ovens, 15
Farmhouses, 15, 34, 36, 42
Fire, avoiding outbreaks of, 89, 124-5
Firebacks, 38
Fireplaces and fireplace surrounds, 17, 37, 40, 54, 70, 77
Firescreens, 38, 78, 119
Floorboards, loose or unsupported, 27; treatment with a sanding machine, 27
Flowerbeds, tendency of to rise against walls, 23
Flues, 54; leakage of fumes from, 124
French polish, 102
Fruitwoods, 27, 76
Furnishing Your Home (1940), 81
Furniture beetle, 22, 63, 101-2

Garden furniture, 109
Garden walls, 108

Gas, mains supply of, 18; bottled, 19, 45; heaters, 54; cookers, 96
Gate-leg tables, 71-2
Georgian grates, 38
Glare, 24
Glass-paned doors, 62
Gothic furniture, 115
Goulden, Gontran, 80
Graining, 120
Guest room items, 89
Gutters, 23-4, 37, 127

Haircord, 30, 55
Handles for furniture, 57-8, 93
Hardboard, as a base for tiles, 30
Harmonious colours, 64
Heat and other marks on furniture, 102
Heated towel rail, 80
Hepplewhite, George, 75
Herbert, A. P., 110
Hob grates, 38, 78
Homes Sweet Homes (1939), 16
Horse brasses, 17
Horse-hair mattresses, 55
Household tools, pots and pans etc, a basic list of, 105-6

Indigenous woods, 76
Inglenooks, 15, 17, 77
Insurance, 21, 124
Inventory, 126
Irons, 125

Joist ends, signs of rotting in, 27
Jumble sales, 41
Junk shops, 41, 63, 73

Kettles, 46
Kitchen ranges, 45, 78
Kitchen shelves, 45
Kitchen units, 43
Kneehole desk, 93

133

Index

Ladder-back chairs, 48
Ladders, to reach bedrooms, 53
Lampshades, 59, 64
Lancaster, Osbert, 16
Larders, 43; turned into bathrooms, 79
Lavatory pans, 81
Lavatory seats, 84
Letterbox, 21
Linen basket, 81
Lino tiles, 29
Linseed oil, 37
Local maps, framed, 90-1
Logs, use as fuel in dining rooms, 71, 77-8
Long hopper (wc pan), 20
Looking glasses, 59, 63, 70, 87, 89
Loudon, J. C., 114-15, 117, 122-3

Mahogany, 17, 76, 98, 101
Mail-order firms, 96
Mantlepiece, 70
Matchboarding, 37
Medicine cabinets, 83; childproof, 84
Methylated spirits, 102
Mice, 21-2, 38
Mirrors, 63, 70, 87, 89
Modern furniture, 48, 67, 72-3, 75
Mouldings, 61-2, 102

Neighbours, 25
Noise, 24
Norfolk latch, 52

Oak, 16, 27, 36, 58, 60, 71, 76
Oil lamps, 19; fitted for electricity, 19
Open fires, 19, 24, 41, 71, 77
Orchard grass and bulbs, 108
Ornaments and pictures, 17-18 32, 37, 40, 65, 77; spare room, 90

Oval tables, 17, 71

Painting floorboard, 27
Panelled walls, 36-7
Papier mâché chairs, 67
Paraffiffin stoves, 81
Parlours, standard size for Georgian, 62
Parquet floors, 29
Party walls, 25
Patchwork quilts, 56
Paving a back yard, 110
Pelmets, 32
Pembroke tables, 66, 71
Picture hanging, 17, 32, 70
Picture rails, 62
Pine, 46, 60
Plastic tiles, 29
Polishes, 32, 37, 102
Pot-pourri, 71
Pull switch for bathroom light, 82
Pump, 20

Quarry tiles, 29

Reading chair, 94
Regency furniture, 67-8, 72
Repairing minor defects in furniture, 102
Reproduction furniture, 48
Restoring Junk (1970), 102
Rising butt hinges, 28-9
Rocking chairs, 58
Roller blinds, 83, 87
Roofs and chimney stacks, 24
Round tripod tables, 51, 65, 98
Rugs, on floors, 29, 55; on walls, 37
Rural Rides (1825), 68
Rush matting, 28-9
Rush-seated chairs, 48, 50

Sealing fluids, 27, 29
Seasoned wood, 63

Index

Secretaire bookcase, 17, 68
Serviceable furnishings for tenants, 127
Sewing tables, 67
Sheds, 110
Sheraton, Thomas, 75
Shower, 79
Sideboards, 75
Side tables, 63
Sinks, 43, 45-6
Skirting boards, 28-9, 83
Sliding doors, 46
Sloping floors, 27
Smoking fireplaces, 24, 38, 125
Sofa-beds, 95, 118
Sofas, 69-70, 85, 94
Sound-proofing materials, 25
Spindle-back chairs, 48, 68
Spinning wheels, 17
Spiral staircases, 30
Staircases, 30, 37, 53
Stair carpets, 30
Stone-flagged and brick floors, 27, 43
Stone-throwers, 16
Storage of food, 46
Suffolk Harvest (1956), 111
Sundials Old and New (1967) 110
Sutherland table, 65

Table lamps, 17, 64
Teak, 76, 109
Telephone numbers useful for tenants, 125
Tenancy agreements, 126
Tenants, 124-8
Threepiece suites, 69
Tiles for bathrooms, 82
Tomrley, Mrs C. G., 81
Tongued and grooved boards, 37
Traffic noise, 25
Typewriter, 93

Upholstery and loose covers, 65, 92, 126

Vases, 17
Ventilation, iron grids for admitting mice, 21; proving if adequate, 24; under-floor, 27; local for open fires, 38; provision of by flues, 54
Victorian grates, 40

Wainscotting, 37
Wallboard, 23
Wall coverings to be avoided, 36
Wallpaper, 36, 48; bathroom, 82
Wall pegs for clothes, 87
Walnut, 76, 101
Warping of woodwork, 63
Washstands, 58, 89
Wasp and bee nests, 22
Water, lack of mains, 19, 58; burst pipes, 24; uncertain local supply, 125
Wells, dangers of, 125
Wet rot, 36
White paint, 30-2, 40
William Morris chairs, 48
Window frames, removal of to let in furniture, 30, 53
Windows, 16; appropriate size for, 24, 61; in bedrooms, 59; in bathroom, 80; in study, 93-4
Windsor chairs, 47-8; 52, 73, 76. 98
Wing chair, 51
Wood blocks to make furniture stand level, 26-7
Woods, mixing of, 76
Woodworm damage, 22, 63, 101-2
White chair, 94
Writing tables, 56, 93

135